ADVANCE PRAISE

Sarah Locke's memoir left me feeling seen and empowered. She masterfully weaves themes of personal acceptance, resilience, and self-advocacy into deeply relatable storytelling. Reading this book feels like an act of self-care, and as Sarah writes, "Self-love is the foundation that makes every step forward possible."

Kristin Key
LQBTQIA+ Advocate and Comedian

Sarah Locke's story is one of strength and unwavering determination. From her journey of self-discovery to navigating the challenges of an MS diagnosis, she has met each chapter of her life with authenticity and courage. Sarah turned personal adversity into a life of purpose and impact, becoming a passionate advocate and influential voice for the MS community. Her commitment to our shared mission to find a cure for MS, along with her relentless push for change, is deeply inspiring. This book is not only a story of resilience, but a beacon of hope for every person affected by MS.

Tim Coetzee, PhD
President and CEO, National MS Society

Over the past couple of decades, I have diagnosed many individuals with multiple sclerosis, and I've seen two paths emerge—those who feel overwhelmed by helplessness and those who turn their diagnosis into purpose, pushing forward to help others in extraordinary ways.

This book is a testament to resilience, courage, and unwavering determination. I have had the privilege of being Sarah's neurologist, witnessing firsthand her relentless energy—not just in facing the challenges of MS but in standing up for those who cannot. Her journey of coming out later in life and navigating an MS diagnosis is raw, honest, and deeply inspiring. Sarah has turned every obstacle into fuel, proving that authenticity and strength go hand in hand. An extraordinary read from an extraordinary human being.

Dr. Ann Cabot, DO
Neurologist, Advocate, and Proud Supporter

There are few people in this world more real, authentic, kind, and resilient than Sarah. Her story, so eloquently told in *Living Out Loud*, is so beautifully multi-layered, especially how she shares her complete commitment to living her life authentically and unapologetically. This book is so uniquely human in sharing how Sarah spent much of her professional life weaving in her coming out story so that other LGBTQ+ people could find happiness through self-love. Because of her example, the workplace is a safer place and a place where the LGBTQ+ community can thrive. Reading this book reminds me why Sarah inspires me every single day to ensure an inclusive culture is woven into corporate culture for the rest of history.

Erik M. Day
Senior Vice President, Dell Technologies
PRIDE ERG Global Executive Sponsor

Sarah's story proves real power isn't physical—it's mental.

A must-read for anyone facing a mountain they believe they cannot climb. It's not about MS or being gay; it's about the human spirit refusing to give up.

This book is for anyone who has been told they can't but is ready to prove they can.

Sarah's story took me on a rollercoaster of emotions and lit a fire in me that I didn't know I had. I laughed, cried, cheered, and closed the book feeling stronger and empowered as an MS warrior.

This isn't just a memoir about MS—it's a triumph of spirit that speaks to each of us. It's a rallying cry for anyone told they can't. Sarah proves that the most extraordinary power is mental, not physical, and her tribe ensures no one fights alone.

And this isn't just a story of surviving MS—it's about finding your truth and living it out loud. Sarah Locke's coming out, her fight with chronic illness, and her creation of Locke's Promise are nothing short of extraordinary. Her vulnerability and strength inspire us to rise, no matter our battle. Sarah's grit, humor, and raw honesty make this a book I'll never forget.

Melissa Cook
Living with MS
Author of *The Call of the Last Frontier:*
The True Story of a Woman's Twenty-Year Alaska Adventure

Sarah's story is raw, brave, authentic, and beautifully unapologetic. Watching you step into your truth as a gay woman, a mother, and a person living with MS illustrates to your readers the power of resilience, love, and becoming. I'm endlessly proud to witness your light.

Julie A. Stamm
Living with MS
Mom; Advocate; and Co-author of *Some Days: A Tale of Love, Ice Cream, and My Mom's Chronic Illness*

Sarah writes with a conversational style that is easy to read and draws us into her story of challenge and change. Her energy radiates from the pages as she remains positive and upbeat while realistic. She describes well what many in the LGBTQIA+ community live with during their adolescent and even early adult years. But "coming out" turns out not to be the only challenge Sarah faces. What is it like living with multiple sclerosis? Sarah shares that, too, because she faces many dragons on her journey.

Charmaine Jones, MD
Living with RA
Director, Dragon Claw Charity LTD (Australia)

LOUD

Living Out

LOUD
Living Out

A MEMOIR OF SPEAKING UP, BREAKING FREE,
AND FINALLY BEING SEEN

SARAH LOCKE

Press 49
4980 South Alma School Road
Suite 2-493
Chandler, Arizona 85248

Volume pricing is available for bulk orders from corporations, associations, and others. For bulk order details and media inquiries, please contact Press 49 at info@press49.com or 833.PRESS49 (833.773.7749).

For more information and to donate to support multiple sclerosis initiatives and Sarah's efforts, visit www.lockespromise.com or reach out to Sarah directly at sarah@lockespromise.com

FIRST EDITION

Library of Congress Control Number: 2025911395

ISBN (paperback): 978-1-953315-57-1
ISBN (eBook): 978-1-953315-58-8

BIO026000 BIOGRAPHY & AUTOBIOGRAPHY / Memoirs
BIO031000 BIOGRAPHY & AUTOBIOGRAPHY / LGBTQ+
SOC029000 SOCIAL SCIENCE / Disability
SOC057000 SOCIAL SCIENCE / Disease & Health Issues
SOC074000 SOCIAL SCIENCE / Diversity & Multiculturalism

Interior and cover design by Medlar Publishing Solutions Pvt Ltd., India

Printed in the United States of America

TABLE OF CONTENTS

ACKNOWLEDGEMENT

Writing this book has been a journey filled with challenges, reflections (both painful and enlightening), discoveries, and an outpouring of love, and I would not have been able to accomplish it without the incredible people who have supported me along the way.

To my daughter, my heart, my everything, and my "why"—you inspire me every single day. Your love, empathy, independence, and strength give me the courage to keep moving forward, even when the path is difficult. Everything I do, I do because of you, and I am endlessly proud to be your mom.

To my ex-husband, thank you for your unwavering kindness, understanding, and support. Your generosity of spirit and our shared commitment to our daughter have been anchors during life's transitions, and I am deeply grateful for the care you've shown me.

To my partner, family, and friends who have stood by me through every twist and turn, thank you for holding me up when I faltered and for believing in me when I struggled to believe in myself. You are my foundation, and your love means everything.

To the MS community, especially those who have shared their stories, challenges, and triumphs with me, thank you. Your resilience fuels my passion, and I am honored to stand beside you as an advocate, friend, and fellow traveler on this journey called life.

To my Locke's Promise family—my incredible board of directors, volunteers, and supporters—you have helped turn a vision into reality. Your dedication and shared belief in creating meaningful change inspire me every day. Together, we are proving that community is a force to be reckoned with.

And finally, to you, the reader of this book, thank you for taking the time to share in this journey. Whether you're living with MS, supporting someone who is, or simply looking for inspiration, I hope you find stories that resonate, uplift, and remind you of the strength within us all.

This book is dedicated to everyone who has ever faced a mountain, whether literal or metaphorical, and found the courage to keep climbing. Thank you for walking alongside me. Together, we are unstoppable.

PRELUDE:
THE STORY BEHIND THE STRENGTH

This is my story—one of transformation, resilience, and authenticity. Every chapter of my life paints a vibrant picture of my world, highlighting the challenges I've faced and the triumphs I've achieved. From growing up on a dairy farm to conquering the summit of Mount Washington, from raising my daughter with unwavering love to founding my own nonprofit, my journey has been one of inspiration and connection.

But my story isn't just about overcoming obstacles; it's about embracing change, even when it's terrifying. One of the most defining moments of my life was coming out as gay at the age of thirty-five. A profoundly personal revelation sent ripples through my family and community. I had built a life I was content with—a loving marriage, a beautiful daughter, a stable home—but I realized I couldn't continue without embracing my authentic self. The decision to come out wasn't easy. It came with guilt, fear, and heartbreak, but it was rooted in love for my daughter and my desire to lead by example. I wanted her to see that it's okay to stand out, to embrace who you truly are, even in the face of adversity.

Coming out was a pivotal step, but life didn't slow down for me after that. Shortly after, I learned that I had multiple sclerosis (MS)—a diagnosis that brought its own set of challenges and uncertainties. Yet, I refused to let fear or illness define my path. My journey became one of self-discovery and reinvention, proving to myself and others that strength lies in vulnerability and authenticity.

The chapters ahead delve into various aspects of my life: my love for adventure and off-roading, my profound bond with my daughter, my candid relationship with social media, and my tireless efforts to raise awareness and funds for the MS community. They uncover moments of doubt, guilt, triumphs, and my relentless drive to create Locke's Promise—a nonprofit born out of my desire to turn personal challenges into collective strength. Every chapter shows that coming out wasn't just an act of courage—it was the beginning of a journey toward living unapologetically as me.

This is a story of grace, perseverance, and transformation. It's a testament to the idea that the most complex challenges, significant changes, and the deepest fears can lead to extraordinary growth. Welcome to my story, one that celebrates resilience and the power of living authentically.

Chapter 1

WHERE IT ALL BEGAN

It's said that everything has a beginning, a middle, and an end, and I believe that to be true. The real question is—where does it truly begin? For me, this journey has many roots. If I were to sum it up, my story unfolded in phases: childhood, college, life as I knew it, coming out, the diagnosis, and beyond.

Each phase of my life carries its own story—every experience shaping the person I am today. Together, they led me toward a purpose and legacy far bigger than myself—a chance to make a difference in the lives of others.

So here we go, diving into what I will refer to as "before the shift" of my life, referring to my coming out. Consider this the abbreviated edition.

GROWING UP: A FARM GIRL WITH BIG DREAMS

I grew up in rural upstate New York, smack dab in the middle of two brothers—the lone girl in our trio—on a family dairy farm. Life was shaped by early mornings, the smell of fresh hay, and an unapologetic tomboy style—baggy jeans, sneakers, and a backward hat were my signature look. I wanted nothing more than to be "one of the boys," proving I could keep up.

Farm life was demanding, tough, and relentless, but I thrived on challenges. My competitive spirit pushed me to prove that I was just as strong as—if not stronger than—my brothers. Whether shoveling manure, feeding calves, or picking up rocks in the fields, every chore tested my grit and resilience.

One of our regular "competitions" centered around pull-ups on the center beam of the barn, though *competition* was a loose term. My older brother would casually jump up, grab the beam, and knock out a few effortless reps before continuing on his way. On the other hand, I had to jump to reach it, my fingertips barely catching hold. I'd strain, pull, and fight for every inch, only to drop back down without managing a single complete rep. And yet, every day, I'd try again, chasing the moment when I'd finally be able to lift myself, just like him.

I knew I would get there one day—I just had to keep trying.

Beyond farm duties, I found joy in showing dairy cattle. It perfectly blended my love for animals and ambition to excel. As a dedicated member of 4-H, I spent years learning cattle judging, honing public speaking skills, and giving back through community service. My peers were busy navigating high school drama. Meanwhile, I focused on leadership, teamwork, resilience, and planting seeds of strength that would later carry me through life's most complex challenges—challenges I couldn't have imagined.

HIGH SCHOOL: THE CHAMELEON YEARS

Though I worked hard in sports like basketball and softball, I knew I wasn't destined to be the MVP. But sports weren't about the spotlight—they were about belonging and being part of something bigger, a team.

Socially, I was a chameleon—able to fit in anywhere but never truly finding a place that felt like home. If "most likely to blend in" were an award, I would have won it effortlessly. While others built deep friendships, I gravitated toward family and cousins, all farmers like me, who understood the rhythm of hard work and quiet determination.

Yet, a lingering question followed me through those years: Who am I, really? Was I meant to fit into every space without fully belonging to any of them? Did I truly know what I wanted, what I stood for, what made me different? Or was I just going through the motions, adapting to whatever was expected of me?

I wondered: Was it better to blend in or stand out? Did I want deep friendships, or had I convinced myself that solitude was easier? Why did I feel at ease in certain moments and painfully out of place in others? Was I holding myself back or simply waiting for the right space to feel seen?

It was an unspoken struggle for which I didn't have the words at the time, but looking back, I see it clearly. It wasn't that I lacked connections—I hadn't yet found the connections that felt truly, unmistakably mine.

COLLEGE: ESCAPE OR EVOLUTION?

College was supposed to be my great escape—a chance to shed the farm girl persona, leave behind manure-scented mornings, and step into who I truly was. Spoiler alert: It didn't quite happen that way.

I chose Clarkson University in Potsdam, New York, chasing my dream of becoming a marketing professional, where I envisioned trading hay bales for skyscrapers, and turning my knack for storytelling into a career.

Clarkson was known for producing engineers who built both literal and figurative bridges. Still, I found my place in marketing, thriving in a business program focused on connection and strategy. By 2003, I had earned both bachelor's and master's degrees in business, thanks to Clarkson's 4+1 program, which allowed me to fast-track my graduate education.

For a girl who once thought cow showmanship was the pinnacle of success, earning those degrees felt like winning gold in the game of life.

LOVE, FAMILY, AND NEW BEGINNINGS

College wasn't just about academics—it was where I finally found my people, the kind of friendships that didn't just fill the time but became the foundation of some of my most unforgettable moments. These friends showed up at three a.m. without question, whether for a full-blown life crisis, a last-minute date rescue, or a desperate "someone come get me—I made a terrible decision" moment.

And then, of course, there were the emergency ice cream runs—because when the craving hit, it wasn't a request; it was a mission. We would pile into someone's car, blasting music that felt way too emotional for the occasion, debating flavors like it was a life-altering decision.

These friendships were unshakable, built on laughter, chaos, and the trust that comes from navigating young adulthood together. College may have taught me plenty in the classroom, but the real lessons? They came from the late-night drives, the ridiculous group chats, and the people who made every moment feel like home.

Even surrounded by them, I hesitated. It wasn't just fear of rejection or disappointing my family—it was the fear of exposing something I wasn't even sure existed yet. I had spent years shifting, adapting, molding myself into whatever felt safest. Blending in had become second nature, and stepping beyond that—revealing something undefined, something raw—felt like an unbearable risk. So I held back, uncertain if I was protecting myself or simply avoiding the truth.

Then, out of the blue, he entered my life during my graduate year of college—someone who saw me fully, even the version of myself I hadn't yet figured out.

I fought against the relationship at first, convinced it wasn't meant to be, even blurting out, "You're not my type"—not realizing how little I actually knew about what that meant. But he was patient. He treated me kindly, respected me, and made me feel seen in a way I had never experienced before.

I may not have known my type, but I knew the kind of person I wanted to share my life with—and he fit that perfectly.

He loved me deeply, unwaveringly, and became my partner in all things. Together, we built a life in New Hampshire, his home state—a place that quickly became ours, a fresh beginning where our story truly took shape.

BECOMING A MOTHER: MY GREATEST ROLE YET

Our family grew—but not without challenges. My body fought me every step of the way, and at twenty-two weeks, complications forced me onto bed rest, stealing any illusion of control I thought I had. Steroids were administered, doctors worked tirelessly, but deep down, I knew—a premature birth was inevitable.

She was my first and only child, yet I was suspended between expectation and uncertainty, grasping at the unknown. People say you never really know what to expect with motherhood, but I wasn't just figuring out the basics—I was bracing for impact. Everything moved so fast, and I was simply along for the ride, powerless against the force of it all.

Let's go back to the word, control. Is it ever truly ours? Or do we just convince ourselves we hold it until life proves otherwise?

Then, during a February snowstorm, she decided it was time. She entered seven weeks ahead of schedule, defied timelines, and instantly reshaped the future. I was rushed to Dartmouth Hitchcock Medical Center in Lebanon, New Hampshire, where she was born on February 20—tiny, fragile, yet undeniably determined.

That moment changed everything. From the second I held her, my world reorganized, centering on creating the best life possible for her. That bond formed in the hospital became

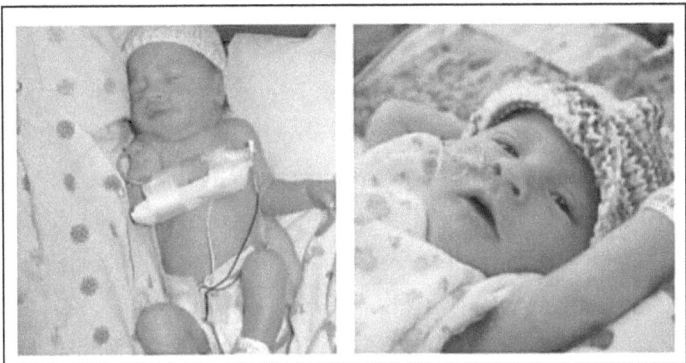

Sarah's daughter, February 2009

the foundation of my relentless drive to overcome every obstacle ahead. She became my why and the reason I would do everything the way I did going forward.

THE VOID I COULDN'T IGNORE

Our beautiful daughter brought light and laughter into our lives, solidifying our happiness as a family. On the surface, everything looked perfect—even picturesque. But deep within, something was missing—something I couldn't name.

It wasn't dissatisfaction with my life, love, or family but a disconnect within myself—like a puzzle with one stubborn piece that refused to fit. I couldn't shake the feeling that something was off. Today, as I write this, "It's me, I'm the problem" keeps entering me head by Taylor Swifts, "Anti-Hero." It only makes sense as the song explores themes of self-reflection and personal struggles, something I often connect to as I relive this part of my journey as I write. I was the problem I just didn't know why, what or how.

CHASING STRENGTH, SEARCHING FOR IDENTITY

As a young mother, my early adult years were shaped by the joy of parenting and my drive to push my limits. I wanted to be strong—not just emotionally, but physically—so I could keep up with my daughter and be the kind of parent who could fully engage in life alongside her. I knew I needed to make a change. I was overweight, struggling with energy, and determined to build a life where I could be active, present, and thriving. So, I dove headfirst into one of the hottest fitness video trends of the early 2000s, committing to a routine that would reshape more than just my body—it would transform my mindset, confidence, and future.

Over time, the weight fell away—more than a hundred pounds gone—but what I gained was even more significant. I became a mother with boundless energy, someone who didn't only feel lighter physically but stronger mentally. That shift propelled me forward, leading me to New Hampshire's 4,000-foot peaks where I wasn't just hiking for the views—I was chasing growth, proving that I was capable of more than I ever imagined.

When hiking wasn't enough, I turned to Spartan obstacle races, pushing my physical and mental limits to new extremes. Crawling under barbed wire, scaling walls, carrying heavy weights, trudging through mud and forest for miles, I faced every challenge with grit and determination. My drive became magnetic, inspiring both friends and strangers alike.

At that point, I was unstoppable. From farm girl to adventurer, mother to competitor, I had built a life of resilience and strength.

Sarah at the Spartan Race, 2015

But I had no idea the biggest challenge of my life was just around the corner—one that would test my strength in ways I could never have imagined.

FROM SEARCHING TO BECOMING

As I referenced earlier, through high school, college, and after, I couldn't quite put my finger on what was missing, if anything at all. I had convinced myself that if I stayed active, got in shape, and kept a positive outlook, the emptiness I felt would somehow fade away. That if I filled my days with movement and optimism, it would miraculously erase the quiet void lingering beneath the surface.

But no matter how much I pushed forward, the question remained: How could I feel so empty when my life was filled with love, amazing people, and everything I had once dreamed of? The answer wasn't in the miles I hiked or the smiles I forced—it was deeper, hidden in places I hadn't yet dared to explore.

This is where my journey truly begins—the moment where "after the shift" takes shape, transforming uncertainty into purpose. Before this shift, I lived in a space of hesitation, carefully navigating a familiar but not fully authentic life. There were expectations, comfort in routine, and an outward appearance of stability, but beneath it all, something was missing—a truth I hadn't yet permitted myself to embrace.

Then, the shift happened. Coming out was the moment that redefined everything. It was a step toward honesty, living without reservation, and becoming the version of myself I had always been but had long suppressed. And while it wasn't easy, while it carried weight and complexity, it also carried freedom.

After coming out, small steps toward change became strides, and resilience evolved into a legacy of authenticity, courage, and self-acceptance. The world didn't suddenly become easier, but it became real, grounded in a life where I no longer had to hide, hesitate, or filter my existence to meet expectations that weren't truly mine.

This next chapter is the beginning of that new reality, the space where I step forward—fully myself, fully seen, and fully determined to keep moving forward, not just for me, but for those who need to know that transformation is possible.

Chapter 2

UNVEILING THE RAINBOW FROM WITHIN

I have learned that our lives are full of necessary pivots, plot twists, s-turns, and challenges. (Did anyone else just say "PIVOT" in the voice of Ross Geller from *Friends*? No? Just me? Moving on.) As I mentioned earlier, the first shift in my life happened when my daughter was born—a moment that changed everything. But the next shift, the one that truly reshaped my identity, came when I finally embraced my truth and stepped into the person I had always longed to be but lacked the confidence to truly let out. It was time.

My daughter became my everything, and I wanted to experience life as she wanted me to—to jump out of an airplane, run with her in a marathon, and ultimately do whatever she wanted me to. It's why I took control of my health after childbirth, losing over one hundred pounds. With fitness came confidence, determination, and most importantly, the courage to confront myself. You might ask, "Why did you need to confront yourself?"

In my honest opinion, confronting yourself during the coming out process is the most crucial step in it all. Before I could seek acceptance from others, I had to accept myself. Coming out wasn't just about telling the world—it was about acknowledging my truth and confidently embracing it. Many people wrestle with fear, doubt, and internalized expectations, but facing myself meant recognizing that my identity wasn't something to be fixed or hidden—it's something to be celebrated. Self-love is the foundation that makes every step forward possible. *Say it with me, "Self-love is the foundation that makes every step forward possible."* Without it, the opinions of others can feel overwhelming, and uncertainty can cloud the journey. But when I chose to love myself first, I created a space where external judgment held less power, my voice became the strongest, and living authentically is no longer a question—it's a commitment to myself.

AND JUST LIKE THAT—CLICK! THE LIGHT TURNED ON

It wasn't gradual, it wasn't subtle—it was instant clarity, like someone flipped a switch in my brain that had been faulty for decades. So it happened. In that moment, I wasn't the same person anymore. The "before the shift" me? Gone. The version of myself that had tiptoed around the truth? Vanished. At thirty-five, the puzzle pieces scattered across my life suddenly fit together.

For the first time, I came out—to myself. And let me tell you, the realization hit like a plot twist in a movie I didn't see coming. I had always known something was missing—a quiet void I tried to fill with movement, achievement, and distractions. But as soon as the truth clicked into place, it was undeniable, exhilarating, and terrifying all at once.

And then, the weight of it crashed down. I cried—deep, gut-wrenching, unstoppable sobs—overwhelmed by the sheer terror of the revelation. It pulled me back to childhood, the fear of rejection, and the quiet moments when I convinced myself that blending in was safer than standing out. But I couldn't shove it down anymore, couldn't pretend. I had finally found the missing piece—that puzzle piece that wasn't lost under the couch or tucked away in someone else's expectations. It had been inside me all along, buried so deep I never saw it coming.

And once I saw it, I had to be me. Authentically. Unapologetically.

Then came the moment that felt like I was standing on the edge of a cliff, heart pounding, knowing there was no way to turn back—coming out to my husband. Of all the steps in this journey, this was the one that felt the heaviest, the most delicate, the most terrifying. How do you say the words that will change everything? How do you break the news that shifts the foundation of a life you've built together? I knew this conversation would take every ounce of courage I had, but there was no more hiding. No more hesitation. It was time.

True to his nature, he supported me completely, lifted me, and loved me through it. Of course, he wasn't happy—his own life was spiraling out of control—but he kept his promise to give me everything I wanted and needed, including unconditional love. Remember that term, *unconditional love*; it plays an important role going forward.

I will always be eternally grateful to him, especially when he stood by my side as I faced our friends and families with this newfound truth. Their reactions were everything I feared and expected—painful, varied, and transformative. Some lashed out, others went silent, and a few quietly accepted.

His family was by far the most accepting and focused on how it all effected our daughter. Even though they saw us both struggling, they knew that since we placed her at the highest of priorities, we would be ok. As I sobbed in their living room, seeing their expressions and knowing this news was both a shock and heartbreaking for them, his father stood up, walked across the room, and did something he pointed out, in that moment, as something he had never done before, even on our wedding day. He hugged me. Relief washed over me. They didn't hate me for who I was; they respected me for my honesty and for being a good mother to their granddaughter. I felt—if only a little—accepted.

The relationships with those who couldn't—or wouldn't—accept me are still being rebuilt, though they'll never quite be the same.

Through it all, I kept moving forward, refusing to let their opinions define me. I finally knew who *I* was, and I wouldn't let anyone squash that.

Change is inevitable—it's the one constant in life. In New England, we often say, "If you don't like the weather, wait a minute," because it's always changing. In your career, they say, "If you aren't changing, you aren't growing."

I realized I had to embrace that same mindset. I couldn't settle for what was working or what others saw as "perfect." I needed to evolve, push forward, and create my path.

While I've left parts of my old life behind, I've gained something more valuable—pieces of my true self. I am the change. I wear a bangle that reads, "Be The Change," and I say it often when speaking to others. For example, I often say, "Be the change you want to see in your community." We can't just sit back and wish it to be better, hope it to be different; we have to take action.

The hardest part of coming out wasn't admitting the truth to myself—it was grappling with the pain I knew it would cause others. Coming out meant facing the possibility of disappointing the people I loved the most, breaking my promises, and dismantling the life I had so carefully built. By the time I chose to embrace my authentic self, I had already created something that looked good in the eyes of others—something that even I believed was solid and comforting. But deep down, it wasn't everything. It wasn't enough. I had settled and wanted more when I realized there could be more.

The fear of hurting others was paralyzing, but nothing weighed heavier on my heart than the thought of losing my mother's love and support. Our relationship had always been close. We called each other daily, and she had been there for me through life's most challenging moments. When I went on bed rest during my pregnancy, she immediately dropped everything and came from miles away to take care of me. Later, when I developed a severe case of mastitis that spread into an invasive infection requiring hospitalization, she rushed back again to help care for my daughter so I could focus on recovering. We had a bond built on unconditional love—or so I thought.

Maybe it's good to add the definition: *Unconditional love* is a selfless and unwavering act of love offered without any expectations or conditions. It's characterized by acceptance, forgiveness, and altruism, where the giver doesn't seek anything in return. It's about loving someone for who they are, not for what they do or can provide.

Coming out tested that bond in ways I could never have anticipated. My mother didn't just struggle with my revelation; she took it personally. To her, it felt like a reflection of her parenting and a disruption of the life she had envisioned for me. Although she knew other people who were queer, the idea that one of her children could be was unfathomable. And when faced with the reality, she broke.

It was devastating. I felt profound guilt, not for my choice to live authentically but for the pain it caused someone I loved so deeply. My mother lashed out, and the situation escalated to the point where I had to block her number and distance myself entirely. She refused to accept my truth, the daily phone calls stopped, and she severed ties on social media, completely withdrawing from the day-to-day storytelling that had once connected us. It wasn't the story she had imagined for me, and she couldn't bear to watch it unfold.

The person I needed most didn't understand and didn't want to try. For the first time, I realized that unconditional love wasn't something my mother could hold above her expectations. There were attempts to change my mind, as if my coming out was a lighthearted, reversible decision rather than a deep personal journey that I had been internally struggling with my entire life. When my mother finally realized she couldn't sway me—and that even my heartbroken husband supported me—she walked away, cutting off all ties, even to her granddaughter.

TIME HEALS

The moral of this part of my story is simple: Healing takes time. I didn't push my mother to accept me. I let her go, understanding that she needed space to process, reflect, and reach her own conclusions. It wasn't easy, and the process wasn't quick. Eventually—and it was a long eventually—we sat down to talk. For the first time, I could share my truth and revisit moments from my childhood that, in hindsight, had pointed to the person I truly was.

Those conversations didn't happen overnight; rebuilding our relationship took years of patience, understanding, and grace. Over time, my mother stopped seeing me through the lens of my identity and, instead, embraced me for the daughter I had always been—full of humor, determination, and love. Conversations became easier, though she never apologized; I've accepted that she doesn't see anything to apologize for. Rather than wasting time trying to change her, I embraced our differences and focused on the bond we still share.

While she may not fully accept that part of me, she recognizes my drive, resilience, and devotion to family. Today, she supports my ambitions, traveling with my dad to one of my biggest events for MS awareness. We stay in touch, reconnecting on social media, returning to our lengthy phone calls, albeit not as often, and she plays an active role in my daughter's life. She is a grandmother and a mother who loves in her own way—and that's what matters most. Our relationship has evolved, shaped by patience, understanding, and the willingness to grow together. In many ways, my love for her has deepened. I have witnessed her struggle, felt the weight of what she's endured, and watched her fight with everything she has to love her daughter fully once more. And now, after all of it, she's here—by my side—again.

This experience taught me a valuable lesson: No one can rush someone else's process. Parents, especially, may need time to reconcile the dreams they once had for their children with the reality of their child's truth. It's a slow journey but one worth taking.

A MESSAGE FOR THE NEXT GENERATION

This experience shaped the way I parent my daughter. I'm determined not to set expectations or impose limits but instead to raise her with no boundaries on being herself. My goal is simple: Teach her to embrace herself without fear, and encourage her to support others in doing the same.

My message is one of unconditional acceptance: Let people be themselves in whatever form that may be. Celebrate them, and be their ally.

My story of coming out isn't just about finding my truth—it's about having the courage to face loss, the patience to rebuild love, and the determination to leave a legacy of acceptance for future generations.

Chapter 3

FACING THE UNSEEN, EMBRACING THE INEVITABLE

In August 2019, four years after coming out and when I finally felt some recovery from flipping my world upside down, my life took an unexpected turn. Out of nowhere, I was diagnosed with MS—an incurable and invisible disease that sent my world spinning. One moment, I was thriving, balancing a successful career with a big tech company and maintaining an active, healthy lifestyle. The next, I was grappling with a diagnosis that would redefine my path in ways I never could have anticipated. It proved that just when you think your plate is as full as it can be, the universe has a way of piling on even more. I was just beginning to enjoy my authentic self, and then this.

At the time, my role at work kept me busy, often taking me on business trips from the West Coast to the UK and very often to Texas. The infamous summer heat there, soaring above

110 degrees, was a test of endurance. During one such trip, I felt strange, unfamiliar unease—something wasn't right. Ever the optimist, I brushed it off with humor, joking on social media that the weather was officially "too hot for Sarah Locke."

But the laughter stopped when I returned home. The morning after my flight, I tried to get up from the couch and realized I couldn't feel anything from my chest down. I stumbled to the floor, my mind racing. My husband and I were separated at the time but still living in the same home. More than just co-parents, we were best friends, fully committed to raising our amazing daughter together. With that explained, we sat, trying to problem-solve why I was on the floor. He laughed and joked that it was way too early to be drinking—a much-needed lighthearted moment in the middle of an experience that carried weight—a weight we would soon learn wasn't going anywhere.

The questions were racing through my mind. Had I injured myself during a workout? Could it be a blood clot from the plane ride? I spent the following week trying to shake it off, pushing through with stretching, swimming, and yoga. Maybe it was just a pinched nerve. Maybe it would pass. But it didn't.

When I finally saw my primary care physician (PCP), things escalated quickly. After a battery of questions and an evaluation of my symptoms, my doctor proposed three potential culprits: Lyme disease, lupus, or multiple sclerosis. None of which I wanted, and my mind went blank. This couldn't be real. What followed was a whirlwind of tests, starting with a thorough Lyme panel and a culmination of MRIs to search for lesions, telltale signs of MS.

The results came in quickly, and so did the life-altering news. I hadn't even made it home from my thoracic MRI when my PCP called: The scan revealed demyelination at my T2 vertebrae. I can still remember her words, clear and direct: "Hi, Sarah. I am sorry to tell you that you have demyelination at your T2. This indicates that you most likely have MS." The numbness, the tightness in my core—it all made sense now. But with the answer came a torrent of questions: What did this mean for my future? Could I recover? Would this get worse?

TAKING CONTROL

Even as the weight of my diagnosis sank in, I knew I couldn't afford to linger in fear or uncertainty. My first step was to find a neurologist, but the earliest appointment was months away. My symptoms were worsening by the day—I was in the midst of an active flare, and waiting wasn't an option.

Determined to take control—*Remember when my daughter came early and my issue with control? Is it even something we ever have?*—I became my fiercest advocate. Every morning at eight a.m., I called the specialist's office, politely but persistently asking for my case to be reviewed. I refused to be just another file in a stack. I believed my story mattered, and the right doctor could help me turn it into a success story.

That persistence finally paid off. Just three weeks after my PCP delivered the life-altering news, my phone rang— Dr. Ann Cabot, a highly recommended MS specialist in New England, was calling me herself. The weight I had been carrying suddenly lifted, and the tears came before I could even process the relief. For the first time since hearing those words—*multiple sclerosis*—I felt like the tide was shifting, like I wasn't alone in this fight. In that moment, I understood that self-advocacy wouldn't just be important—it would be my greatest ally on this lifelong journey.

I met with Ann the next day to review my MRIs and outline a plan. She officially diagnosed me with relapsing-remitting multiple sclerosis on September 6, 2019, a day I will remember fondly as the day I got answers—the day that I met the team of doctors that would help me take back control of my life, or as much control as medically possible. She walked me through the necessary steps, from immunizations to managing symptoms. To halt the active flare, she prescribed a five-day course of intravenous steroids starting immediately. With a clear direction and treatment plan, I felt an unfamiliar but welcome emotion: hope.

STRENGTH IN SUPPORT

Managing my physical health was only half the battle. Emotionally, I leaned heavily on my hiking tribe, family, and best friends—the people who had been with me on every mountain I climbed—literally and figuratively. Now, they stood by me as I faced a challenge unlike any before.

One friend, in particular, became my anchor. As a staff member at the hospital where I saw my doctors, she managed to bypass the usual restrictions and accompany me into the infusion center during my intravenous steroid treatments. On my first day there, I sat alone in a sterile room, trying—and failing—to hide my fear. Her calm presence and smiling face immediately

Christy Learn
MS you say? Challenge accepted. All in. Educated.
Determined. Positive. Hopeful. Fire in her eyes.
Laughing and making the best of the cards that have
been handed to her. One of the strongest people I
know. MS should fear her... All of the things that run
through my head as I listen to her talk about her
diagnosis and treatment options. Thanks for letting
me join you...like you got a choice 🙄💜 #Bethestorm
— with **Sarah J. Locke**.

SEP 13, 2019

Sarah's anchor and friend's Facebook post, September 2019

eased my tension when she walked in. She didn't bring solutions
or grand promises; she brought herself. Her companionship
reminded me I wasn't alone, and for the first time that day, I felt
like I could do this. Whatever "this" ended up being.

At one point, I couldn't help but ask her, "Why me? Why
did I work so hard to lose weight, to be the best mom I could

be for my daughter, only to have this happen?" She paused for just a moment before replying. "Because you are the kind of person who will pick yourself back up and make a difference in the world." Her words landed with a force I hadn't expected. In that moment, I realized my diagnosis wasn't a full stop—it was the beginning of a new chapter.

THE FORK IN THE ROAD

Thanks to my friend's encouraging words, I may have known that I could make a difference in the world, but that didn't mean I was always emotionally strong. I realized strength isn't just about pushing forward—it's about navigating the moments when everything feels like it's falling apart.

When I think back to that day in September 2019, I remember my diagnosis arriving like a thunderstorm on a summer afternoon—swift, chaotic, and utterly uninvited. One moment, life felt manageable, and the next, I was sitting on my couch, gripping the phone as the words *incurable disease* echoed in my mind, looping endlessly. My world, which I had just begun reorganizing after the upheaval of coming out, suddenly felt fractured again. But this time, it wasn't just a missing puzzle piece or two—it was as if someone had dumped the entire puzzle onto the floor, scattering everything I had worked so hard to piece together.

At first, there was denial. Surely this couldn't be real. Maybe they had mixed up the results or missed something obvious. I clung to the hope that I'd wake up and realize it had all been a bad dream. But as I read through pamphlets, medical journals, and my MRI results with cryptic notes from my doctor, the truth began to sink in. My diagnosis wasn't going anywhere. This was my new reality.

Then came the grief—the kind that didn't just hurt but consumed me from the inside out. It wasn't only about the disease itself; it was about losing the version of myself I had fought so hard to find. The person I had just started to know and truly love—the one who effortlessly hiked mountains, laughed with her hiking tribe until her cheeks ached, and made plans without hesitation. That vibrant, carefree, unstoppable Sarah felt like she was slipping away, leaving behind a void I had no idea how to fill. I found myself cycling through the stages of grief— not in a neat, linear fashion but in a messy, looping pattern. There was sharp and searing anger aimed at the universe for its cruelty and randomness. Why me? Why now? I spent days consumed by "what ifs" and "if onlys," wishing I could somehow bargain my way back to normalcy. Other days, depression wrapped itself around me like a heavy blanket, making even the simplest tasks feel impossible.

In those moments, it was easy to let the diagnosis define me. To see myself not as Sarah, the bright and capable woman I'd always been, but as Sarah, the sick person—the one who needed help, the one whose life would never be the same. It was a dark and lonely place, and I teetered on the edge of letting it pull me under.

REDEFINING RESILIENCE

But I wasn't the kind of person to stay down for long. One day, after yet another bout of tears, I looked in the mirror and realized something profound: I still had a choice. The diagnosis may have taken control over some aspects of my life, but it couldn't dictate my spirit. That was mine and mine alone.

With my inner resolve and the unwavering support of my medical team, family, and friends, I began to understand that while MS might change my life, it didn't have to define it. Yes, the road ahead would be challenging, but I wasn't traveling it alone. My diagnosis became the catalyst for a new purpose: turning this challenge into an opportunity for growth, advocacy, and strength.

So I decided to stand up. To take the broken pieces of my life and start building something new. Was it going to be easy? Absolutely not. But I refused to let the illness consume me. Instead, I resolved to make it my purpose—my mission—to find a cure in my lifetime.

The first step was education. I became an avid visitor of National MS Society (NMSS) websites and forums since the organization was known as a trusted source of truth for anyone navigating life with MS. I dove into their research and others, even coming out of different countries, not just to understand my condition but to grasp how it affected others. I joined support groups and forums, connecting with people who shared similar struggles. Through their stories, I discovered that no two experiences were alike—each person's journey with this disease was as unique as their fingerprint. In fact, you'll sometimes hear it even referred to as the "snowflake disease," as no two snowflakes are alike.

I had the incredible opportunity to become one of the first MS Ambassadors for the NMSS—a role designed to reach niche communities and markets that the broader organization might not typically engage with.

As an ambassador, I'm trained and deeply knowledgeable (or able to get the answers) about all things MS, and my mission is to bring that awareness to my community in an engaging, impactful, and action-driven way. From hosting unique events that foster connections to raising critical funds for research and support, my role is about making a real difference.

It's about turning awareness into action—bringing people together, creating conversations, and ensuring that no one facing MS ever feels alone. Want to get involved? Join the movement, make an impact, and be part of something bigger! Contact me.

I began speaking out, not only about my incurable disease but also about my whole journey, sharing my story with honesty and vulnerability. I'd share in work employee resource groups, blog about it, and post pieces on social media and in support groups. At first, it was terrifying—opening up about something so personal and painful. But as I spoke, I saw how my words resonated with others. People began to approach me, thanking me for giving voice to emotions they couldn't articulate. I realized that I could empower others to do the same by embracing myself, including my illness. I created a podcast titled *Your Story Is Your Strength: Own Your Story, Share it Often*. My mission wasn't just about educating people about the disease itself. It was about showing them how to support those affected, even if they didn't fully understand. I taught my friends and family that it wasn't about finding the perfect words or offering unsolicited advice—it was about being present, listening without judgment, and simply saying, "I'm here for you."

Of course, there were still hard days. Days when the pain or fatigue was unbearable, or the grief resurfaced like a ghost from the past. But I learned to give myself grace—to acknowledge the difficult emotions without letting them define me.

Over time, I came to see my diagnosis not as an ending but as a new beginning. It forced me to reevaluate who I was and what I valued. It taught me resilience, compassion, and the importance of finding joy in the small, everyday moments.

Most importantly, it showed me that while life might not always go according to plan, it was still worth living—and living fully.

In time, I found myself in an unexpected place—*grateful* for MS's role in shaping my journey. What once felt like an unforgiving diagnosis became the force that uncovered my deepest strength, my unwavering determination, and the advocate within me—one who would not only stand up for myself but fight for countless others walking the same path.

MS didn't just challenge me—it transformed me, pushing me to step forward, speak more loudly, and connect more deeply with my community. It became why I expanded my reach within my hometown and beyond into surrounding towns, where I became a relentless force for change.

That passion led me to create Locke's Promise, Inc.—a beacon of hope for those living with MS. It was never just about awareness; it was about building a movement, a safe space, a lifeline for those who needed it most. What I once considered an insurmountable challenge became my calling, purpose, and reason to push forward.

MS didn't break me—it built me into the compassionate, determined, and unshakable person I am today.

FORESHADOWING THE FIGHT: CONNECTING LIFE'S CLUES

Looking back at my journey, the threads seem to intertwine with an almost eerie precision. As a child, the sun was my nemesis. While other kids basked in its warmth, my body waged war. Any extended time in the heat or direct sunlight left me dangerously ill, shaking from sudden chills in the evenings, doubled over with nausea, or plagued by pounding headaches. Even with religious sunscreen use and no signs of sunburn, my body behaved like it had endured the harshest scorch. It didn't make sense then, but decades later, when a 110-degree week in Texas triggered my diagnosis of heat-intolerance MS, those childhood experiences suddenly clicked. Was it an early warning sign, a foreshadowing of what lay ahead?

The mysteries didn't stop there. In college, I battled a severe case of mononucleosis, brought on by the Epstein-Barr Virus. The illness landed me in the hospital, leaving me exhausted and frail. Little did I know that the virus, dormant but lingering, might have sown the seeds for what would become the trigger to my MS years later. Had the relentless Texas heat reawakened the virus, flipping the switch on my waiting illness? No one can say for sure, but the dots, in hindsight, seem almost too aligned to ignore.

And then there was my battle with endometriosis, a shadow that had loomed over my reproductive health for years. After the birth of my daughter, it grew worse, forcing me to decide to undergo a hysterectomy. Even then, the endometriosis returned, spreading to other areas. In an unexpected turn, once I started treatment for MS—a journey I'll delve into more in the next chapter—the symptoms of my endometriosis nearly disappeared. It was a surprising, unintended benefit of a medication meant to combat an entirely different battle. As I pieced together my history, I began to notice patterns. MS and endometriosis often coexist, part of the web of autoimmune diseases that sometimes travel in pairs or clusters. My mother's struggle with Crohn's disease and endometriosis mirrored my battle with MS and endometriosis. While science hasn't yet proven these conditions to be hereditary, the shared experiences within my family painted a compelling picture of autoimmune connections.

When seen individually, the challenges to my health seemed like isolated fragments. But now, as I reflect, it's as though an invisible thread has been weaving them together all along. Each struggle, each diagnosis, each breakthrough has led me to where I am today—a woman who has turned her hardships into purpose, connecting the dots not just for myself but for others navigating similar paths.

Chapter 4

A LEAP OF FAITH

Going back to when I was officially diagnosed with MS in 2019, there were options provided to me, choices to be made, and hard decisions to be considered. The decision to begin a disease-modifying treatment (DMT) for MS was not one I took lightly. It felt like standing at the edge of a high dive, staring into murky and unknown waters. Drugs for MS offered the promise of slowing the disease's progression, but they came with a steep cost—physically, emotionally, and mentally. These treatments worked by targeting my immune system, suppressing it just enough to stop it from attacking my own body. But this suppression also left me vulnerable, exposed to infections and illnesses my body might once have fought off with ease.

I couldn't help but be wary. Putting such potent drugs into my body felt like a betrayal of the care I'd always taken with my health. The thought of deliberately weakening my immune defenses was a terrifying paradox. Yet, I knew I had to make a choice. I was young, strong, and determined to fight this disease with everything I had while I still had the vitality to stand up to it. Ignoring treatment meant risking an unpredictable future, one where MS might take more from me than I was willing to surrender.

But that didn't make the decision easier. With every brochure I read and consultation I attended, the potential side effects loomed large. MS DMTs can cause a range of side effects such as infusion reactions, increased risk of infections, fatigue, gastrointestinal issues, mood changes, and, in rare cases, more serious complications like progressive multifocal leukoencephalopathy, a rare, often fatal, neurological disease, or cancer, making careful monitoring and individualized management essential…and as I already stated, scary as hell! Some even list "potential death" at the end. Have you ever listened to those commercials where they read the side effects of the drug really fast? I think that's why.

With that said, it was a leap of faith, one that required me to confront my fears head-on. Ultimately, I chose to start with Ocrevus®, reasoning that the strength of the treatment matched my own determination. The infusions were draining, the risks daunting, but I persevered, finding comfort in knowing I was doing all I could to take control of my health. *There is that word* control *again*.

Just months after my diagnosis, the world changed in ways no one could have predicted. The COVID-19 pandemic swept in like a tidal wave, and for me, it was a collision of fears. A disease-modifying treatment meant my immune system was effectively on pause, and a global virus with no clear end in sight left me deeply anxious—an entirely unfamiliar feeling for someone who had always been grounded and level-headed.

I made the decision to close myself off from the world, retreating into my home for what would become nearly three years of isolation. I rarely ventured out, and when I did, it was with an N95 mask and carefully planned precautions. Each outing felt like a calculated risk, a delicate balance between protecting my health and maintaining a sliver of connection to the outside world. Social engagements became a rarity, and even then, I was selective, carefully weighing whether the reward of seeing loved ones outweighed the risks to my health.

The years of isolation weren't without their toll as anxiety became a constant companion. But they also brought clarity. I realized that taking care of myself—my health, my emotions, my boundaries—wasn't selfish. Prioritizing my health during COVID was an act of survival, and moving forward with immune-compromising MS therapies was, too. Choosing to step into the unknown with my treatment was an act of courage, one that demanded trust in myself and my choices. While the journey was anything but easy, I found strength in knowing that every difficult decision I made was a step toward a future that I refused to let MS dictate.

As time went on, my MS journey evolved. I call it a journey because every day is a new adventure with MS. Your symptoms change—you feel great one day and not so much the next. It's like a game of roulette. You wake up in the morning and wonder what the day will bring. With the evolution of my disease, I transitioned from the first MS DMT, Ocrevus®, to Kesimpta®, a new treatment that offered me a slightly different approach to managing the disease. It was a reminder that even as I navigated the challenges, I was never standing still—always adapting, learning, and fighting to maintain my quality of life.

The leap of faith into treatment tested my limits, but it also affirmed my resilience—a reminder that even in the face of uncertainty, I could rise to meet the challenge. For me, it was more than a choice about medication—it was a declaration that I would not be defined by my diagnosis.

Chapter 5

BUILDING A LOVE ROOTED IN COMMUNICATION AND GROWTH

Just as I was learning to navigate the shifting terrain of my MS journey, adapting to new treatments and embracing resilience in the face of uncertainty, another profound transformation was unfolding—one rooted not in medicine but in love, vulnerability, and the deep understanding of what it truly means to grow alongside someone else.

I didn't fall for her because she was perfect—because who is? Love isn't about perfection; it's about finding someone who amplifies your strengths and stands steady when you stumble. It was because she was vulnerable—raw and unguarded in a way I had never encountered before. There was a depth to her that drew me in, a quiet complexity that made me want to learn everything about her. She came with her own mental health struggles, and while those challenges could be daunting, they also made her human. I admired her strength to carry her burdens while still finding the will to love and be loved. It was a completely new experience for me, this feeling of empathy and understanding, and the need to not just share a life but to provide a solid foundation for hers.

I won't pretend it's been easy. During our time together, we've both had to learn and grow as individuals and as a pair. One of the most important lessons I've discovered is that there are things people have to overcome on their own. As much as I want to help her, to shield her from the pain and struggles she faces, I've learned that my role isn't to fix everything—it's to stand beside her and let her find her own strength. That doesn't mean we don't lean on each other. It means that our love has boundaries, and those boundaries help us thrive.

We've come to understand that boundaries and limitations aren't weaknesses—they're tools for success. They aren't about shutting each other out; they're about protecting the relationship and allowing both of us the space to be who we are. She has taught me that boundaries allow us to grow without compromising the love between us. In many ways, we've redefined what it means to share a life together: We don't have to do everything as a unit. She can head out to rock hunt or chase stunning photos of the aurora late at night, while I embrace my passions—jeeping with my friends, spending time with my daughter, and advocating for MS. These moments apart don't diminish our bond; they strengthen it.

Clear communication has become the cornerstone of our relationship. Through therapy, I've realized that bottling up my feelings does neither of us any favors—something I became an expert at from the very beginning of my life, through fear that I would be rejected for my queerness. Bottling things up had become second nature. I had to learn how to let it out and, even though scared, how to communicate through the fear. I've had to learn to express myself, to share the moments that upset or frustrate me, even if it's difficult. She can't adjust or change something she doesn't even know is bothering me, and vice versa. Communication is a skill that we've both had to master. Holding grudges only breeds resentment, and so we've learned to be open, honest, and straightforward with each other.

You've heard me mention "therapy" a few times now. Therapy was never something I thought I would need, let alone embrace. When I first started, it was during one of the most pivotal moments of my life—when I came out. I needed a sounding board, someone who could help me navigate how I was feeling, how to respond to others, and most importantly, how to keep my daughter's well-being at the forefront through it all.

I share this because, like many, I was raised to believe that therapy was for the weak, the broken, the people who couldn't handle life on their own—and to be any one of those things was wrong. But here's what I know now: That belief is harmful, outdated, and entirely false.

Therapy isn't for the weak—it's for anyone looking to understand themselves better, to grow, to heal, to be heard. It's a resource, a tool, a safe place to process life's hardest moments. Before, I never would have labeled myself as having a mental illness, but I do. And rather than hide from it, fear it, or feel shame—I own it. I take action. I do the work.

So, yes, I go to therapy, and I am proud of that. I embrace my struggles because they don't define me, but how I face them does. Therapy has helped me learn how to communicate better, truly listen, manage severe anxiety, and step back into the world after COVID. It has given me skills, self-awareness, and the ability to live my life with more clarity and confidence.

So, if you're struggling, feel lost, or are not sure where to start, therapy is a place to begin. Don't be ashamed. Be proud. Be brave. You are strong, you are empowered, and you deserve support.

I'll admit, being in a relationship with a woman comes with its own unique set of challenges, and having a therapist in these moments doesn't hurt. Women bring high emotions to the table, a depth of feeling that's both beautiful and complex. With both of us carrying those high emotions, it can sometimes feel like we're navigating uncharted territory, especially since we've both fought hard to be who we are. But that passion, that refusal to compromise who we are as individuals, has also been the force that keeps us moving forward. Pushing us to adjust, compromise, and find ways to navigate the challenges without losing sight of what brought us together in the first place.

We found each other on social media during the start of the pandemic, when we were both scared, pulling away from society for our safety and sanity, yet seeing her share her story in a Facebook community, sharing her talent of photography, and using herself as the subject, it pushed me to make a comment, four simple words: "I like your content."

The photo was a picture of her, wrapped in a pride flag, sitting in the middle of a field, looking off into the distance. It was four words that were meant to be a subtle flirt but nothing too heart-wrenching if she didn't get what I was

Sarah's partner, 2019

laying down…but thankfully, she picked it up and we started messaging each other.

If you recall earlier, I described my life as missing pieces, like a puzzle.

It turns out I wasn't just missing a single piece—she was one of quite a few. With her, the puzzle finally started to come together, and for the first time, I found the person who fit me.

The person who stands by me even in my toughest moments. She's the one who reminds me to listen to my body, even when my instincts tell me to push through the fatigue one more time. She loves me for who I am and understands me in ways that make our relationship thrive. She's the one who, when I get hot while hiking and need to cool off, won't skip a beat but will snap a picture and then join in so I don't feel alone.

Sarah, 2020

Sarah and her partner, 2020

And on a whole different extreme, when I suddenly lose the motivation to go for walks—a routine we both enjoy—she doesn't take it personally. She knows it's not her; it's me navigating my energy reserves, figuring out how to get through the day. Instead of being hurt by my "no," she goes for a walk on her own, embracing the independence we've built into our partnership.

We've learned to celebrate our individuality while standing side-by-side. She loves supporting me, sharing my story, and helping me reach my highest potential. At the same time, she encourages me to embrace the passions that fuel me just as I do for her. Our love isn't built on the need to always be together; it's built on trust, respect, and the mutual understanding that we are stronger as individuals who choose to be a team.

Sarah and her partner, 2021

I fell for her not just because of what she shares with the world but because of who she is behind it all—unyielding, determined, and unapologetically herself. She has worked tirelessly to become the person she is, never letting anyone define her or alter her truth. Even though we don't always see eye to eye on certain beliefs, she gives me the space to hold my own, stand firm in who I am, and never questions my right to do so. Loving her isn't about grand gestures or singular moments—it's the sum of all the ways she shows up. She asks, "How can I help?" rather than assuming; she listens, absorbs, and then rises, time and time again.

My partner is funny—though, let's be real, not *quite* as funny as I. She has a way of drawing people in, commanding a room when she wants to, but she's just as content curled up with a book, journaling her thoughts, and sipping a perfectly steeped cup of tea. She chases solace under the stars and somehow manages to make the night sky look even more breathtaking, as if she and the universe have an understanding—one where beauty, peace, and a little quiet magic are meant to be shared.

Kathryn Stockett wrote, "You is kind. You is smart. You is important." That is her—kindness in how she loves, intelligence in how she moves through the world, and an importance that comes from the sheer force of her resilience. She will not be broken. She is mine, just as I am hers. And on the hardest days, when the weight of the world feels unbearable, I will carry her as she has carried me because together, we are enough.

She is compassionate in the way she loves—with open arms and without conditions. Caring, not just in gestures, but in how she listens and understands before offering solutions. And she is a quiet reckoning—steadfast, unshaken, and a force that doesn't demand attention but earns respect simply by being who she is. She moves through life with strength and grace, not seeking approval but radiating the kind of presence that commands it. She lifts others without hesitation and stands tall in her truth, proving that resilience doesn't always roar—it sometimes whispers, unwaveringly and in an unstoppable fashion.

So, no, relationships aren't easy, but they're worth the effort, especially this one! I've learned that love isn't about avoiding frustration or conflict—it's about growing through it. We still get frustrated, we still have to compromise, but we approach those moments with honesty and respect. She's my partner, my supporter, and my safe space. And while the road ahead will always have bumps, we're committed to walking it together—communicating, growing, and thriving.

And if I'm being honest, that's how every relationship should be. Don't be afraid to share your real feelings with your partner—it will only make them understand you better.

Chapter 6

BALANCING LOVE AND BOUNDARIES: CREATING HARMONY IN A BLENDED FAMILY

With the addition of my partner entering my life, it also meant she was entering my daughter's life. This is where I learned that navigating a blended family dynamic can be both rewarding and challenging, especially when balancing different roles and expectations. My partner has a strong desire to take on a parental role in my daughter's life, but for me, it's not necessary. This isn't about dismissing her love or care—it's about recognizing the unique relationships already in place and ensuring that everyone feels valued, understood, and supported.

Sarah with her family—daughter, partner, and Zephyr, Summer 2022

PRIORITIZING STABILITY AND CONNECTION

My daughter has an incredibly involved father and me—two parents who love her wholeheartedly. She doesn't need another authoritative figure, but she does need trust, support, and a stable, harmonious environment.

While my partner sees parenting as part of her role, this has sometimes led to tension between her and my daughter, and differences in parenting styles have sparked conversations between the two of us. Thankfully, co-parenting with my ex-husband has been strong and balanced, allowing us to raise our daughter as a united front. As she approaches college in just a few short years, my commitment to being the most supportive mom I can be remains unchanged, ensuring she has a solid foundation and healthy relationships with the people closest to me.

SHIFTING PERSPECTIVE THROUGH THERAPY

Because I'm learning to ask for help when I need it, I brought these concerns to my therapist, who offered guidance that reshaped my approach to this situation. They explained that fostering a strong relationship between my partner and my daughter is not about authority—it's about connection, trust, and understanding.

Instead of stepping in as a parent, my therapist encouraged me to define the role differently—one of a trusted, supportive friend rather than an authority figure. Research supports this approach, particularly when both biological parents are actively involved. Allowing my partner to build a meaningful friendship with my daughter creates harmony, reduces tension, and fosters a healthy dynamic that benefits everyone.

We're still working toward complete harmony, and it's a daily journey—but one worth taking. Stress is a major trigger for my MS, and balancing family, relationships, and personal well-being requires intentional effort. That's why I rely on research, therapy, and real-life experience to guide my decisions.

Blended families require patience, honesty, and understanding—there's no perfect roadmap, but I know that balance and respect are key. For me, that means preserving my daughter's relationship with both her parents, ensuring my partner

Sarah with her daughter and partner, August 2022

feels respected and valued, and fostering open conversations that keep us moving forward.

This chapter of my life is about nurturing connections without creating conflict—about building a future rooted in trust, love, and harmony. No matter what challenges arise, my priority remains the same: to create a family dynamic where everyone feels supported, appreciated, and understood.

NAVIGATING ILLNESS, ISOLATION, AND THE JOURNEY BACK TO THE WORLD

The pandemic forced a dramatic shift in my life, as I think it did in many. Once filled with jet-setting across continents for work, I suddenly found myself grounded, isolated, and adjusting to a remote world. While I missed the energy of airports, face-to-face meetings, and new experiences, working from home became a sanctuary—a way to continue my career while protecting my health.

With MS and a suppressed immune system, every outing carried risk, making remote work feel like an unexpected gift. But as restrictions lifted and travel became possible again, I faced a new challenge—how to reenter a world that no longer felt familiar.

Therapy played a crucial role in navigating this transition. It helped me process my fears, advocate for my needs, and build confidence in taking necessary steps—whether requesting hotel rooms on ground floors, minimizing exposure, or leaning on my network for support. My colleagues went above and beyond to accommodate my concerns, reinforcing that I wasn't alone.

Ultimately, working remotely taught me adaptation, while my return to limited travel reinforced the importance of advocacy—both for my health and my ability to continue thriving in my career. Today, I still feel most comfortable working from home, but I embrace opportunities to venture out when needed, always balancing safety, career, and well-being.

BECOMING A NINJA

Even as the world started venturing back out in early 2022, I wasn't ready. Crowds? No, thanks. I felt safest masked up, steering clear of people entirely. But let's be real—I can't sit still for long. I needed something new, something that let me move, grow, and challenge myself while still respecting my limits.

Enter Yogi Flight School—a program my cousin introduced me to in the summer of 2023 that focuses on flexibility, core strength, and balance through light, mindful movements. No intense cardio, no brutal climbs—just movement that felt good and made sense for me. Living with MS had already taught me the importance of listening to my body, and the idea of short but meaningful workouts clicked in a way that felt exciting rather than overwhelming. It wasn't about conquering mountains anymore—it was about finding balance, one mindful movement at a time.

Having already adjusted my emotional and nutritional balance to shed weight and reclaim my health, I wanted to take the next step—learning to move with purpose and to support my body in ways that would serve me for years to come. Though I was excited, I had my doubts. Yoga seemed daunting—an activity requiring fluidity, strength, and grace, I was convinced my body wasn't built for. "Too big, too heavy, and entirely incapable," I thought. But as I soon discovered, those were just excuses waiting to be dismantled.

With my cousin's encouragement, I dove into the free five-day online sessions offered by the program. Skeptical but hopeful, I wanted to see if I could break past my limitations. To my amazement, I quickly learned arm balances like the lunge, crow, and flying pigeon—and, shockingly, I found myself enjoying every moment. It wasn't just about the physical movements; it was about preparing my body, warming up properly, and embracing the process. I felt as though I was flying, my confidence soaring alongside my newfound abilities.

Yogi Flight School wasn't just about learning yoga—it introduced me to a philosophy I could integrate into every aspect of my life. The program called its participants "ninjas," a title I proudly embraced. It wasn't just about mastering poses; it was about learning, growing, and becoming more focused and stable in every area of my life.

I quickly fell in love with the community surrounding the program. From live online sessions to an extensive library of classes, I found myself immersed in a supportive environment full of like-minded individuals. The Facebook group offered encouragement and camaraderie, reminding me that I never had to face this journey alone.

LESSONS LEARNED

For me, the true value of the program went far beyond physical benefits. It instilled a newfound confidence in my abilities, challenging me to rethink not only my limitations but also my mindset. Weekly emails from the instructor posed thought-provoking questions and themes that extended beyond yoga. One recurring theme—commitment—struck a deep chord with me.

The instructor shared personal stories and reflections, asking participants to consider what they were truly committed to. I realized I had often been committed to my limitations, viewing them as immovable obstacles and adopting a martyr-like mindset. But commitment, I learned, was a choice—one that could be redirected toward authenticity, freedom, and growth.

One powerful concept introduced in the program was the "Oh Shit" moment—that pivotal instant when doubt creeps in and failure feels inevitable. I learned to embrace those moments, trusting that my body, properly warmed up and prepared, could handle the challenge. These moments weren't just limited to yoga; they became a metaphor for life itself. Whether balancing on my arms or navigating personal struggles, I found strength in pushing through my fears.

NINJA IN THE WILD

My commitment extended beyond the mat. Inspired by the program's adventurous spirit, I began challenging myself to perform yoga moves in the wild—on the mountain tops I reached

Sarah holds a crow pose atop her dad's tractor, August 2022

after arduous hikes. My favorite pose, the crow, became a symbol of perseverance and balance. Each time I succeeded, it brought an undeniable smile to my face—a testament to my ability to steady my body and achieve what once felt impossible.

Some days were harder than others. There were times when the poses didn't come together, when the effort felt overwhelming. But I never stopped trying. Living with MS meant that every victory, no matter how small, was worth celebrating. I committed to the process, understanding that the benefits extended far beyond physical fitness. It was about how the practice made me feel—strong, capable, and alive.

My journey into yoga wasn't just about becoming a ninja on the mat; it was about becoming a ninja in life. With every pose mastered and every "Oh Shit" moment embraced, I learned that balance wasn't just a physical act—it was a state of mind. And while the handstands and grasshopper moves might still elude me, I remain steadfast in my commitment to practice, grow, and soar.

THE POWER OF A PUSHUP

Yoga has taught me the power of mindful movement, balance, and breath, but when it comes to pushing my physical strength, nothing beats the simplicity and challenge of a solid pushup session. There's something incredibly satisfying about testing my endurance, feeling my muscles engage, and knowing that every rep builds both power and resilience. Therefore, this book wouldn't be complete without talking about my love for pushups—and my uncanny ability to stick to them like a morning ritual. Pushups aren't just a workout for me; they're a mindset, a reminder, and most importantly, a daily declaration of my strength, both physical and mental.

Pushups, as I'll proudly tell anyone who asks, are an incredible strength-building exercise. They engage the arms, shoulders, chest, core, and even the legs, providing a full-body workout packed into a single movement. From wide hands to staggered, elevated feet to fast-paced variations, I experiment with every style I can, keeping my routine fresh and challenging. But just as with yoga, the power I find in pushups goes far beyond their physical benefits.

Every morning, I hit the floor and commit to ten or fifteen pushups—rarely skipping a day, unless the universe throws me a truly exceptional reason. For me, it's as much about the act as it is about the intention. I approach each set not as a chore but as an opportunity to center myself, reflect, and affirm that I can still move, still push forward.

The magic in a pushup isn't just physical for me—it's mental and emotional, creating a connection between my body and my mind. Often, I'll set a goal for each pushup or dedicate each repetition to something I'm thankful for. "It's not just about strength," I often say. "It's about the reason behind the movement."

THE POWER OF PUSHUPS—MORE THAN MOVEMENT

My relationship with pushups is almost poetic. Whether I'm on a dock as the lake stirs awake or atop a mountain I've conquered with grit and determination, they've become more than just a workout. They're my daily reminder: I still can.

What started as a simple exercise has transformed into a practice of discipline, resilience, and accountability. Over time, I've built strength—not just in my arms and shoulders but in my resolve. I keep things interesting by experimenting with variations—slow and controlled reps, explosive movements, wide or narrow hand placements, and advanced challenges like Water Bugs. This constant evolution fuels my motivation and ensures that my routine never feels stagnant.

But the real power of pushups isn't just physical—it's mental. Every morning, when I hit the floor and complete my set, it's a testament to showing up for myself. These moments of movement reinforce my determination, reminding me that big results come from the small acts performed repeatedly with intention and persistence.

While many people chase grueling workouts and high rep counts, I've chosen a different path—ten pushups a day. It may seem minor, but that consistency has been transformative. It brings me clarity, blood flow, and a spark of accomplishment that carries through the rest of my day.

No matter where I am—whether in my living room, on a mountain top, or just needing an unexpected boost of confidence—pushups are my anchor. They remind me that strength isn't just about muscles; it's about commitment, accountability, and the choice to keep going.

So, yes, there is power in a pushup—far beyond its physical benefits. It's a daily practice of determination, a celebration of strength, and a reminder to the world (and to myself) that I am ready to own this day.

THE WEIGHT OF BROAD SHOULDERS

It's a common thread woven throughout this book: I possess grit, determination, and an unrelenting refusal to give up. These traits weren't handed to me—they were forged in the fire of my life experiences and shaped by hard lessons, monumental challenges, and small victories that collectively made me who I am today.

"Scared? No worries. Follow me." It's a phrase I live by. Throughout my life, I've shown that fear isn't the absence of strength—it's the crucible that forges it. Whether it's standing up to societal expectations, climbing mountains (both literal and figurative ones), or challenging myself to become the best version of who I can be, I've always led by example. My mantra is as simple as it is profound: *Do the hard thing. You'll be better for it.*

I often joke that I was born with broad shoulders so I could carry the weight of the world—and in many ways, that's true. My life's challenges—being the lone girl in a family of boys, feeling isolated during my formative years, navigating the struggles of coming out—all tested my strength. But they also taught me how to stand tall, even when the weight of the world felt overwhelming.

My journey isn't just a story of resilience; it's a testament to the power of authenticity, grit, and determination. I hope my example can shine as a beacon for anyone feeling the weight of their own struggles. I've shown that it's possible to carry that weight, push through fear, and emerge stronger and more true to yourself than ever before.

Chapter 7

GRACE UNDER PRESSURE: MANAGING STRESS, STRENGTH, AND THE REALITIES OF LIVING WITH MS

I have talked about stress a few times already, but it's a key factor in my life now. Stress is often dismissed as a fleeting emotion or a natural part of life, but for me, living with MS—it's so much more than that. It's a trigger, an unpredictable force that can turn a manageable day into one filled with fatigue, pain, and cognitive fog. It's a stark reminder of the deep connection between the mind and body—how emotional strain can manifest in physical ways I can't always control.

The science behind it is undeniable. Stress activates the body's fight-or-flight response, flooding it with hormones like cortisol and adrenaline. While this can help in moments of immediate danger, prolonged stress throws everything out of sync, weakening the immune system, increasing inflammation, and worsening my MS symptoms. Each flare-up tells me that I'm not just battling the disease itself—I'm battling stress, too.

Managing stress has become a pillar of my survival. But it hasn't been easy. I've always been fiercely independent, someone who prides herself on tackling life head-on. Slowing down? Asking for help? Those things didn't come naturally to me. Yet, MS forced me to reevaluate how I approach my well-being. Self-care isn't optional—it's essential.

I now find solace in mindfulness practices—meditation, deep breathing, and small daily rituals that keep me grounded. The simple act of sipping tea in the morning, journaling, or walking in nature reminds me that life doesn't have to be about pushing full speed ahead. I can pause. I can breathe. I can choose balance.

But finding balance is complicated when strength and determination have been at the core of who I am. If you ask me how I manage to keep going through pain and fatigue, I'd probably shrug it off—it's just what I do. Movement has always been my way of fighting back. I move for my daughter. I move to lead by example. Giving up simply isn't an option.

I joke that I was built to be a machine, but the truth behind that humor is real—I rarely stop. When I first shared my MS diagnosis with colleagues, I asked for one thing: grace. I warned them that fatigue might hit hard, that words might occasionally slip away. A co-worker, half-jokingly, told me, "Well, thank goodness Sarah was born with the energy of ten people. Now, with MS, she might just be normal."

The reality, though, is that even when I seem composed—put together, energetic, and relentless—I eventually crash.

My body forces me to stop. You might find me answering emails from bed, too exhausted to sit up, but refusing to fully step away. Those closest to me have seen it happen on the hardest days or long hikes when my legs feel too heavy to lift, when even my smile struggles to stay in place.

The problem with strength is that people assume it's endless. But I am not invincible. My determination is often in service of others, ensuring they have the best experience, even if it comes at my own expense. The truth is I need grace, too. I need people to notice when I should slow down, when I need help, even if I won't ask for it myself.

At my core, I am a mother, a leader, and an example—proof that fear, pain, and fatigue can slow me down, but they will never stop me. And yet, as MS forces my body to redefine movement, I have had to find new ways to keep going. So, I turned to four wheels because no matter the challenge, I will always find a way forward.

FINDING FREEDOM ON FOUR WHEELS

The next phase of my journey has been about movement—not just physically, but mentally and emotionally. MS may have slowed my steps, but it hasn't diminished my drive to stay active, productive, and engaged in the world around me.

I once conquered towering mountains and covered long distances with ease, my legs carrying me across ten to fifteen miles of rugged terrain in a single day. Now, my hikes have shifted to two to three miles on flatter paths, my body's limitations forcing me to reimagine what adventure looks like.

But rather than mourning what I've lost, I've found new ways to embrace the thrill of exploration.

And that's where off-roading comes in—the answer to my restless spirit. It's a way to keep moving, chase the feeling of discovery, and prove that even when the journey looks different, it can still be exhilarating. This chapter is defined by adaptation, resilience, and the refusal to let obstacles stand in my way.

It all started, unknowingly, just a few months before my diagnosis. While driving home after a Mother's Day meal with my daughter and ex-husband, we passed a dealership with a gleaming black Jeep Wrangler Rubicon parked out front. Without hesitation, I exclaimed, "Stop! I need that!" My ex-husband, playfully teasing me for perhaps being mildly intoxicated from a Mother's Day lunch out filled with celebratory drinks, dismissed it as impulsive. But the idea didn't fade. The next day, I called the dealership, scheduled an appointment, and went to take a closer look.

When I saw that Jeep again, I just knew—it was the one. I couldn't quite articulate why, but it resonated deeply with me. It wasn't just a car; it was freedom, empowerment, and a symbol of stepping into my own independence. It became my first major purchase as a newly separated woman—a declaration of autonomy. To some, it might have looked like a midlife crisis at thirty-nine, but for me, it was something I simply had to do.

Little did I know that, in a matter of months, I would lose sensation in my legs, and my days of summiting 4,000-foot mountains would become rare occasions. I couldn't foresee then how much that Jeep—fondly named Hashtag, a nod to my social media branding—would come to represent a lifeline.

Sarah's Jeep Wrangler, a 2017 Rubicon Recon JKU, named Hashtag

THE CONNECTION GROWS

From the moment I was diagnosed, I made one clear proclamation: No matter what adjustments or modifications it required, I would always be able to drive Hashtag. This Jeep wasn't just a vehicle—it was a symbol of my independence and my refusal to let MS define or restrict me. Even before I fully understood why, I felt empowered behind the wheel, as though Hashtag and I were forging a new path together.

What began as a casual interest in off-roading evolved into a deeper connection when I joined a Facebook group for women Jeep owners. It was a tentative step toward finding a community, but one that paid off. Through this group, I discovered the Jeep Girl Mafia Club—New Hampshire Chapter, an all-female off-roading collective that changed my life.

A NEW ADVENTURE BEGINS

From the very first event, I felt a profound sense of belonging. This wasn't just a hobby group—it was a sisterhood, a space where I could be myself without judgment or limitations. Off-roading became more than driving on dirt roads—it was about building connections and reigniting my adventurous spirit.

I fondly recall my first off-roading adventure with my daughter. The event, hosted in Vermont, promised a light and easy ride through covered bridges and along scenic dirt roads. Neither of us knew quite what to expect, but we arrived to find a group of thirty Jeeps, their drivers, and their pit crews. It was a match made in heaven—I had found my new outlet.

The experience was a revelation. Off-roading offered me a way to explore the world's beauty in a way that was accessible, exciting, and fulfilling. The Jeep Girl Mafia Club's supportive spirit only deepened my love for the activity. Every ride wasn't just an adventure; it was a reminder that I could still chase thrills, build friendships, and push boundaries—even in the face of MS. As I grew more confident, I tackled more difficult trails and obstacles, transforming Hashtag into a machine I knew could get me anywhere. Hashtag's tagline became #TakeMeToTheMountains as I turned her into my accessibility vehicle.

REDISCOVERING JOY

My journey with Hashtag transformed what could have been a painful loss—the shrinking ability to hike high mountains—into a new and empowering passion. With my Jeep and my new community by my side, I found a way to keep moving forward, proving once again that where there's grit, there's a way.

With Hashtag as my partner in adventure, I fell in love with the rush of adrenaline that came from tackling off-road trails. I learned to navigate rough terrain, from conquering rocky paths to mastering mud and water crossings. Each outing was an opportunity to enhance my skills, test Hashtag's capabilities, and immerse myself in the thrill of the moment. For me, the exhilaration of the outdoors didn't come from expending physical energy—it came from embracing the challenge, strategy, and camaraderie of the off-road experience.

Modifying my Jeep became another cherished aspect of my passion. Spending time researching the best parts, deciding what was needed for specific trails, and customizing Hashtag gave me a sense of control again—something I worried MS might take from me. Hashtag became my sanctuary, a space where I could feel free and capable, even on days when my body didn't cooperate.

The Jeep Girl Mafia Club brought me more than adventures—it gave me a community of like-minded women who lifted each other up, shared laughs around campfires, and cheered on one another through every obstacle, both on and off the trail. It reminded me that I didn't have to navigate my challenges alone. With Hashtag, my skills, and the encouragement of my newfound tribe, I rediscovered joy and a sense of purpose in simply getting out there and living life my way.

Hashtag in the mud, 2023

Hashtag off-roading, 2024

Hashtag rock crawling, 2024

Chapter 8

THE POWER OF CONNECTION

For me, social media isn't just a tool—it's a lifeline. In today's ever-connected digital world, platforms like Facebook, LinkedIn, and Instagram have become vital spaces where I make meaningful connections, stay in touch with those I care about, and amplify my voice to spread awareness about MS. What started as a simple channel to share updates has transformed into a dynamic way for me to educate, inspire, and build a community of hope and resilience. It's also how I make connections on a professional level. Leaning into my LinkedIn network is how I found my publisher. Having no idea where to begin, I reached out to people who did, and that introduction was a testament to the power of social media.

Social media is where I tell my story—authentically and transparently. For me, it's not about curating a perfect image or "selling" myself. It's about sharing real moments, the highs and the lows, and connecting with others on a human level.

My posts offer glimpses into my life: snapshots of my advocacy efforts, my love for Hashtag the Jeep, my daily pushups, my unwavering battle with MS, and yes, even the occasional photo of my skillfully plated healthy meals that look almost too good to eat. But I always remind my followers that what they see online is just one layer of the story. As open and honest as I am on these platforms, my life runs much deeper, filled with complexities and experiences that can't be fully captured in a caption or video.

Let me jump back for a moment to highlight a powerful example of how social media can drive impact and shift perspectives. When I came out, people's concern wasn't just about me—it was overwhelmingly focused on my ex-husband. While I was trying to focus on my own journey, the questions kept coming: "How is he?" "Is he handling this okay?" "He must be so depressed." And when I answered with "He's okay, we're working through this together as a team," that wasn't enough—people kept digging for more.

After discussing it with him, we decided to take control of the narrative in a way that would lighten my burden. Since my audience was on social media, we agreed that he—someone who rarely posts—would share his own perspective. (And yes, I can hear you saying "Aww" out loud—he really is an amazing man, and my dad was right—I chose him for a reason.)

He took his time, crafting a thoughtful, intentional post—one that would reshape how people viewed our relationship and this transition. And truly, the only way to fully experience it is to read his words for yourself.

Nearly fourteen years ago I met someone who would change the trajectory of my life forever. Sarah J. Locke (nee Russell) burst into my life like an atom bomb and as I tried to reassemble myself I found some important pieces missing. It didn't take long to realize those pieces now lived in her and that I couldn't be complete in her absence. A few years later I was fortunate enough to marry the woman who had become my very best friend.

I recognized from the beginning that she, too, had some pretty important pieces missing. I know that I held some of them, but there were still some missing, and through the years, we've managed to find more of them together. In the past several months, we found a really big one, and it has dramatically changed the trajectories of both our lives. That's the reason I'm writing this letter to all of you today.

Before I get to that, though, I want to tell you about my best friend. She has a fire inside her like no other. We all carry a flame that propels us forward in life, in all the things we do. Sarah carries a raging inferno. Her drive and determination and commitment to all that she pursues [are] unmatched. We've all witnessed the latest endeavors in her health and fitness. Many can attest to the equal commitment she makes in her professional life. And I can attest to the unwavering, unconditional love and care that she provides our wonderful daughter. In everything Sarah sets her mind to, she is an unstoppable force.

My best friend makes me laugh. She makes everyone laugh. When the two of us get together, it sometimes gets so intensely funny that we can't even form coherent words through laughter and breathlessness. This is a gift beyond value. It is said that laughter is the best medicine. If true, she is a healer of the highest order.

Another of her defining qualities is a desire for truth. She expects it from everyone around her and so elevates us all to greater virtue. It played a transformative role in my own personal development over these years and it is an unimpeachable model for our daughter. And this truth isn't just about being honest with others, and in your actions. Most importantly, it is about being true to oneself. Everything else follows from that.

Sarah has enriched my life in countless other ways, big and small. Every moment I spend with her makes me want to be a better person, for myself, but most importantly for my family. Above and beyond and before everything else, we are family. Forever. No matter the path she travels. And that brings me back to what this letter is all about.

Sarah Locke is my family, no matter what else has changed. She is my very best friend. She is the mother of my daughter. She is an inspiration. She is my hero. I will always love her. And she is gay.

And the responses to his post (as well as the ❤ emojis!) were beyond anything I could have ever imagined. Here are a few of them.

Tricia Carter Gagne:
I've never met you in person, ..., but I feel like I know you through Sarah. The journey you share is truly inspirational, especially for those [who] do not have the same ability to be as honest and raw as you have. [Redacted] is very lucky to have both as parents.

Maura Karhnak Froshour:
Wow, thank you for loving and supporting her! Best friends are so important, and no matter what the road has in store for both of you, you have created a lasting, loving

family, friendship, and partnership. Sarah is blessed to have you support her as you have We ♥ u Sarah; you are family to us as well!!!

Krista Curtis Dounetos:
Amazing!! Just amazing...!!! Thank you for loving my cousin unconditionally and being such an amazing example of love for her and [redacted]!!!!! Sarah is one of the most inspirational people I know!!! She and [redacted] are so very lucky to have you!!! ♥

Keri Racicot Bresaw:
This is the epitome of unconditional love and of the purest foundation of truth in a relationship. I love you two so much—what an incredibly strong couple and incredible individuals. Blessed to have you in our lives—we should all be so honest and true to ourselves and those we love. You are absolutely beautiful people—in every aspect of that aesthetic.

Marybeth Hobbs Stramaglia:
The way the two of you have faced this life change is truly an inspiration. I am sure that it has been painful in many ways, but the love, understanding, friendship, and support are just breathtaking in the best possible way! ♥

Mari Devitte:
Got me crying over here like a baby at noon on a Friday, man! You guys are great parents and people, and we're all here to support you no matter what! #loveislove.

Was I right? Social media's impact speaks for itself. Hundreds of comments, and even now, people continue to engage as it resurfaces in their memories on Facebook. That's the true power of social media—delivering a message that resonates and sparking conversations that create real change.

BUILDING BRIDGES

One of the most remarkable aspects of my relationship with social media is how I use it to forge connections. It's not just a way to broadcast my message; it's a two-way street where I learn from others, discover new perspectives, and build genuine relationships. Through my posts and engagements, I've met like-minded individuals who share my passion for advocacy, and I've even found myself inspired by the stories of others.

Social media has also become an essential tool for my non-profit, Locke's Promise. It allows me to promote events like Climb the Peak for MS, the MS Golf Classic: Swinging for a Cure, and Rides & Wranglers for MS; attract donors, participants, and sponsors; and reach a wider audience with my mission. By staying active and transparent online, I've been able to grow my community and bring more people into the fold, whether as supporters, volunteers, or friends. Social media has given me the platform to share my story, amplify awareness about MS, and build a network rooted in hope and resilience.

EDUCATING AND INSPIRING

Perhaps most importantly, I use social media as a platform for education. Living with MS has given me a unique perspective, and I'm passionate about using my voice to increase awareness and understanding. Through my posts, I not only share my personal journey but also provide valuable insights into what it's like to live with a chronic illness. I celebrate the small victories, acknowledge the struggles, and break down misconceptions about MS—all with the hope of creating a more compassionate and informed world.

My followers often tell me how refreshing it is to see someone so raw and unfiltered online. In a world where social media often gets a bad rap for being inauthentic or overly polished, my approach serves as a breath of fresh air. For me, it's not about being perfect—it's about being real and showing up as my true self.

A REAL CONNECTION

My presence on social media highlights the balance between authenticity and privacy. Those who follow me catch glimpses of my life, but the full depth of my journey can only be understood by diving deeper—something I hope this book will offer.

Chapter 9

SOBRIETY AND SELF-DISCOVERY

Just as social media became a tool for connection and self-reflection, so did my journey toward sobriety—a path that challenged me to confront habits, redefine comfort, and ultimately step into a new sense of clarity and purpose.

For years, alcohol was woven into my daily routine—a crisp IPA after a long day, the warm embrace of an old fashioned marking the transition from chaos to calm. It felt like a reward, a way to reclaim some normalcy in an unpredictable life. But slowly, what started as a celebration became a habit, and eventually, a crutch.

As I adjusted to life with MS, I began noticing subtle but undeniable changes in how alcohol affected me. At first, I brushed it off, joking that if MS benefited from leafy greens, then hops should also count. I convinced myself that my drinking didn't need to change—if anything, it could become a more accepted indulgence.

But reality doesn't cater to denial. Fatigue arrived faster, the brain fog stuck around longer, and I started to realize that my nightly drinks weren't helping me unwind—they were keeping me stuck. What had been occasional became routine, and that routine was leading me somewhere I hadn't meant to go—toward isolation, dependency, and quiet depression.

If I'm being completely honest, it wasn't just a habit—it was an escape. A way to blur the edges of reality, to drown out the chaos of a workday, the imperfections of a life that refused to fit neatly into place, the weight of an incurable disease that lingered in the background of every moment. It started as a distraction, then became a routine, and eventually, drinking wasn't just unwinding—it was forgetting.

The wake-up call came on a winter afternoon, during a mother-daughter ski day. A day filled with adventure ended as it often did—with a couple of drinks at the slope-side pub. Let's highlight the word *couple*, and let's be real that they happened throughout the day. My daughter was patient as we sat in the snow at the edge of the parking lot, waiting until I was clear-headed enough to drive. She didn't say anything, didn't express frustration, but the weight of that moment settled deep. I wasn't reckless or careless—but I was slipping. The line between a casual drink and something more concerning had blurred.

That moment wasn't just about me. It was about her—the person I care about more than anything in this world. It forced me to acknowledge what alcohol was quietly stealing: my presence, my energy, my ability to be fully engaged with the life I was building.

Sobriety wasn't about giving something up—it was about taking back my power. It proved that I could still find peace, release, and joy without relying on a drink to get me there. Choosing to walk away from alcohol meant choosing clarity, connection, and control—not just for myself, but for my daughter, my future, and the person I am becoming.

At a time when everything felt uncertain, taking control of my drinking became a powerful declaration—a choice that still fills me with a sense of accomplishment. I own my sobriety completely, and that's something worth celebrating. Kudos to everyone reclaiming their path!

THE DECISION TO CHANGE

The realization was both a wake-up call and a moment of clarity. I could no longer ignore what alcohol was doing—not just to my body, but my mental and emotional state. Living with MS demanded that I listen to my body and make thoughtful choices about what I consumed. But alcohol had become an anchor, pulling me further from the person I wanted to be.

So, I made a change.

Be the change you want to see in yourself.

Quietly and purposefully, I decided to cut alcohol out of my life. I didn't frame it as a grand, sweeping declaration. For me, it was simply another step in the ongoing journey of understanding how my body works with MS and what it needs to thrive. I vividly remember the date I gave up alcohol. That day became more than just a personal milestone; it symbolizes transformation, resilience, and possibility. I celebrate that anniversary every year to inspire others who feel trapped by their habits or self-doubt. My message is simple yet powerful: If I can do it, so can you.

THE BENEFITS OF SOBRIETY

Almost immediately, I began noticing the changes. Without alcohol in my system, my energy levels stabilized, and the ever-present fatigue I had blamed entirely on MS started to lift, even if only slightly. The mental fog that once clouded my evenings dissipated, leaving me with a clearer sense of purpose. Mornings, which had often begun sluggishly, became opportunities to start fresh, unburdened by the effects of the night before.

More importantly, I found myself reconnecting with the things that mattered most. Evenings that had once revolved around a drink became moments of reflection, creativity, and connection. I enjoyed deeper conversations, explored new hobbies, and felt more present in my interactions with my daughter. My decision wasn't just physical; it was emotional, mental, and deeply empowering.

Research has shown the benefits of sobriety for individuals living with MS, and I've experienced them firsthand. Alcohol can exacerbate common MS symptoms like fatigue, cognitive fog, and poor coordination—issues I was already battling. Removing it from my life gave me a greater sense of control, both over my body and over my daily routines. It was a choice that allowed me to approach my health with the same grit and determination that has defined every other aspect of my life.

Chapter 10

A NEW PATH FORWARD

Sobriety wasn't a finish line; it was another step in my journey of becoming the best version of myself. It was a choice rooted in love, resilience, and the unwavering belief that every challenge, no matter how difficult, could be met with courage and grace.

But grace, I've learned, isn't always easy to give to myself. There were moments when doubt crept in—I questioned whether I was strong enough, whether slipping up meant failing, or whether I could truly rewrite the habits I had relied on for so long. It wasn't about perfection; it was about progress, about allowing myself to grow, stumble, and keep going without self-judgment.

Some days felt effortless, like I was fully stepping into the clarity and freedom I had been searching for. Other days tested me—times when I longed for old comforts, when stress whispered that one drink wouldn't hurt, when the weight of responsibility felt overwhelming. In those moments, I reminded myself that choosing sobriety wasn't about restriction; it was about liberation—liberation from patterns that no longer served me, from foggy mornings and restless nights, from relying on something outside of myself to feel okay.

Grace meant forgiving myself for the hard days, celebrating the small wins, and recognizing that healing isn't linear. It meant embracing that growth takes time, patience, and self-compassion. It meant reminding myself that I was worthy of this journey, that my decision to step away from alcohol wasn't just about removing something—it was about creating space for something better.

I've come to see sobriety not as deprivation but as an act of self-love, a commitment to showing up fully for myself and the people who matter most. And through this, I've learned that grace isn't just what I offer to others—it's what I must offer to myself, again and again, as I keep choosing the life I know I deserve.

Chapter 11

A SUMMIT OF HOPE: TURNING DETERMINATION INTO LEGACY

Just as sobriety was an act of self-reclamation, proving that I could rewrite old habits and step into a new version of myself, my journey with MS became another test of resilience, strength, and purpose. This challenge pushed me to survive and take action, make an impact, and turn my determination into something far greater than myself.

I think we can all conclude by now that my diagnosis didn't silence me—it amplified my voice. I was determined to raise awareness about MS, not just to share my own story but to foster understanding and community. I refused to let MS define me, and I knew I had to take action in a meaningful way.

Fueled by this newfound purpose, I launched a fundraiser for the National MS Society, setting an ambitious goal of $10,000. Instead of simply asking for donations, I tied it to something deeply personal—a bucket list challenge I refused to let MS take from me. I would hike Mount Washington, the tallest peak in the Northeast, a test of endurance that mirrored the mountains I was climbing in my own life.

It would take place in June of 2020, during the isolation of the COVID-19 pandemic. I trained for the ascent, rallying my hiking friends—my tribe—who had been beside me through countless adventures. When hike day arrived, we hit the trailhead at five a.m., carrying determination, humor, and the unwavering commitment to keep moving forward.

The climb was brutal. My body protested every step, but the encouragement of my friends kept me pushing ahead. We rested when needed, soaking in the camaraderie and drawing strength from one another. Mount Washington's notorious, unpredictable weather could shift from sunshine to raging storms in mere minutes, so every step demanded vigilance.

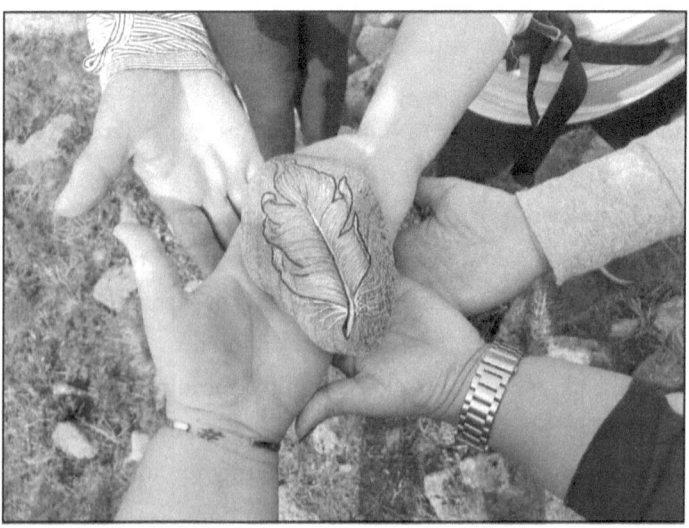

Rock painted with MS-inspired feather left on Mount Washington, 2020

At one of our stops—a quiet pond nestled between peaks—I pulled a rock from my pack, one that carried deep personal meaning. A friend had painted an orange feather on its surface—orange for MS awareness, a feather for letting go, and the rock itself represented the weight of my diagnosis. I placed it on the shore, tears streaming down my face. It was a symbolic release, a moment of defiance. As I turned to continue the climb, I whispered, "FU, MS," leaving my burdens behind.

When I finally reached the summit, emotion overwhelmed me. I stood at the highest point in the Northeast, surrounded

Sarah looking at the climb ahead during her MS Awareness Hike up Mount Washington, June 2020

Sarah and her anchor and friend, embracing in tears as they are about to summit, June 2020

by the friends who helped me get there. My body ached, but my spirit soared. The diagnosis that once felt like an impossible mountain was now just one more challenge conquered.

Rather than taking the planned in case of emergency, relief vehicle down, I chose to descend via the Jewel Trail, the most

Sarah at the Summit of Mount Washington, June 2020

grueling descent I had ever faced. The rugged terrain and the fact that I had already given all I had to reach the summit made for one of my most difficult descents. But I did it. And just as exhaustion settled in, drenched in sweat and drained from the effort, I received the news: My fundraiser had reached $10,000.

Standing at the base, I realized this wasn't the end of my journey. It was only the beginning. If I could raise $10,000 on my own, what could an entire community achieve? The seed of something bigger than myself had been planted. It wasn't just about my story anymore—it was about building a movement, turning determination into a legacy of hope.

CLIMBING TOWARD A STRONGER FUTURE: TURNING CHALLENGES INTO COMMUNITY

After conquering Mount Washington, I felt a familiar pull—the urge to keep going and find the next challenge that would not only push my limits but raise awareness for MS in a meaningful way. My journey has never been about standing still; it's about proving that life with MS is not defined by limitations but by the ways we choose to face them. Whether scaling mountains, embracing my Jeep community, or committing to daily pushups, my story is about perseverance, not as a singular act but as a way of life.

But this time, I wanted my next challenge to be bigger than me. Reflecting on my journey, I realized how impactful it had been to rally around a goal and work toward something with purpose and connection. I wanted to create an event that others could join, something that wouldn't just raise money but build a movement. That's when the idea for Climb the Peak for MS was born.

Pats Peak had always been a special place—a mountain that felt like home, nestled in the heart of my community, filled with adventure and possibility. It was the perfect venue for my vision: an annual climb, bringing people together to conquer the mountain, celebrate strength, and raise awareness for MS.

I shared my idea with Pats Peak, laying out my goals and personal connection to the mission. My passion was contagious, and the venue quickly came on board as a sponsor, helping turn this vision into a reality. Planning the inaugural climb was no easy feat—I was new to fundraising, navigating sponsorships, event logistics, and community outreach. I poured my heart into it, even investing personal funds to bring it to life. But I wasn't alone. My hiking tribe, friends, and local community stepped up, offering their time, ideas, and encouragement to make the event successful.

The day of the first Climb the Peak for MS was electric. Hikers of all ages and abilities gathered at Pats Peak, filled with excitement, purpose, and camaraderie. Standing at the base, dressed in my signature bright orange—a bold symbol of MS

Sarah speaking to the twenty-eight attendees at the first Climb the Peak for MS event, May 2023

awareness—I gave a heartfelt speech, sharing my journey and the power of community.

The mountain filled with conversations, encouragement, and shared determination as we climbed. Every step wasn't just about reaching the summit but overcoming obstacles together. People traded stories, uplifted one another, and found strength in the collective mission.

Reaching the peak alongside friends and fellow climbers, I looked out over the familiar landscape, filled with pride and hope. This event wasn't just a fundraiser but a testament to what can be accomplished when people unite for a greater cause. Climb the Peak for MS proved that no literal or metaphorical mountain was too great to overcome with the right team by your side.

That first climb was just the beginning. Over the years, the event has grown, gaining local press attention, securing sponsorships, and building momentum. It has become more than just a fundraiser—it's that movement I've been talking about, inspiring people to take action in their own ways and empowering the MS community in ways I never could have imagined. In it's third year, and including my original $10,000 from my Mt Washington hike, we have totaled just shy of $100,000 raised for the National MS Society. Our participation has grown from the 28 friends it's first year to over 160 participants this year and several highly involved sponsors!

Looking back, I realize I was laying stepping stones to something bigger, bolder, and brighter, not just for myself, but for everyone affected by MS. And I'm just getting started.

Chapter 12

A VISION BEYOND FUNDRAISING: TURNING ADVOCACY INTO ACTION

As my passion for advocacy grew, so did my ambition to make a greater impact in the fight against MS. My fundraising efforts—fueled by a determination to promote awareness and support research—led me to forge a deeper connection with the National MS Society (NMSS). While my work as a third-party fundraiser was celebrated, I realized that my vision extended beyond raising money—I wanted to create meaningful change for individuals living with MS.

By the third year of Climb the Peak for MS, my name had become synonymous with hope and determination within the MS community. As an MS Ambassador, I had built a reputation for creativity and drive, constantly searching for new ways to inspire, uplift, and empower those navigating life with MS. My frequent conversations with the NMSS became a source of encouragement and collaboration, helping generate greater funds, wider-reaching initiatives, and deeper connections.

It was during one such conversation that they made a suggestion that changed everything: *What if I established my own nonprofit?* This shift would allow me to amplify my efforts, independently manage initiatives, and expand beyond fundraising to provide direct, personalized support to those affected by MS.

The idea resonated deeply. While funding research for a cure was essential, I knew immediate needs were going unmet—needs I could help address locally and personally. Founding a nonprofit wasn't just about giving myself more freedom to create change—it was about building a lasting movement designed to uplift, support, and develop tangible resources for the MS community.

This pivotal step marked a new chapter in my advocacy journey—not just as a fundraiser or ambassador but as the founder of a mission-driven organization committed to making a real, measurable difference in the lives of those impacted by MS. And we shall call it Locke's Promise.

Locke's Promise, Inc.

Chapter 13

LOCKE'S PROMISE: A LEGACY OF STRENGTH, ADVOCACY, AND HOPE

Locke's Promise is built on two fundamental pillars: the unwavering strength of community and the transformative impact of advocacy and awareness. For me, these aren't just abstract ideals—they are the driving forces behind my mission to support and empower those living with MS.

From the beginning, I understood the profound value of community. My hiking tribe, close friends, and newfound connections in the MS world became my lifeline through the darkest moments of my diagnosis. Their support reminded me that no one should ever have to face MS alone, and this became the heart of Locke's Promise—creating a network of tangible support for those navigating the complexities of life with a chronic, invisible illness.

Locke's Promise is more than a friendship circle—it's real help. I envisioned providing resources to ease the physical and financial burdens of living with MS, from making homes and cars more accessible to alleviating the stress of medical expenses. Stress, I know firsthand, can trigger MS flares, making daily life even harder. My goal was to create a space where people could breathe more easily, focus on their well-being, and feel supported every step of the way.

But beyond practical aid, Locke's Promise is a platform for advocacy and awareness. I've been an MS Ambassador with the National MS Society (NMSS) for years, using my voice to educate, dismantle stigma, and inspire action. Awareness isn't just about visibility; it's about changing the narrative, ensuring MS is understood, and securing the support necessary to create meaningful change.

Through Locke's Promise, I've amplified my advocacy efforts, ensuring that MS isn't just a misunderstood condition but a widely recognized, supported cause. My nonprofit has partnered with the NMSS to continue funding research for a cure while directly impacting lives at the local level. My team and I host educational events, share resources, and connect newly diagnosed individuals with others who can guide, reassure, and uplift them.

Locke's Promise exists because I know what fear and confusion feel like. I remember the isolating weight of my diagnosis—the questions that had no answers, the uncertainty that left me grasping in the dark. This nonprofit is my way of saying, "You are not alone. We will guide you, support you, and fight alongside you."

TURNING VISION INTO REALITY

I imagined Locke's Promise as more than just a nonprofit—I wanted it to be a safety net, offering practical tools alongside the emotional reassurance that life with MS could still be rich, meaningful, and fulfilling. The idea for the nonprofit was sparked by the encouragement of a dear friend during my darkest moments—"You don't have to do this alone." If you recall, through this entire book, there were moments and times I felt alone or learned that I wasn't alone. A chronic illness like MS can most definitely make someone feel alone, like no one gets it. Those words stayed with me, shaping the mission of Locke's Promise.

One moment, in particular, solidified its name and purpose. My doctor, MS specialist Ann Cabot, mentioned how she had always wanted to see the phrase "Never MS Alone" printed on a T-shirt. Without hesitation, I responded, "Consider it done." That phrase became the tagline of Locke's Promise, a bold declaration that no one should navigate MS in isolation.

BUILDING A LEGACY

Locke's Promise is more than just a name—it's a commitment to the MS community and their families. I pledge to take action, to make an impact, and to lead with empathy. It's the resource I once desperately searched for but ultimately had to create for myself.

I leveraged my marketing expertise, my fundraising successes with Climb the Peak for MS, and the relationships I had cultivated within the MS community to turn this vision into reality. Locke's Promise isn't just a passion project—it's my legacy.

A BEACON OF HOPE

From fundraising to advocacy to community building, Locke's Promise represents my hope of making a direct impact. It's a force for change, inspiring others to join me in supporting and uplifting the MS community.

Locke's Promise fulfills two goals: fighting for a cure while also addressing the immediate needs of those living with MS. It has become a beacon of hope, proving that life with MS doesn't have to be defined by struggle—it can be transformed into a source of strength, connection, and possibility.

For me, this is my purpose—not simply to face MS, but to use my experience to uplift and empower those who need it most.

Chapter 14

BUILDING LOCKE'S PROMISE—STARTING A NONPROFIT

Starting a nonprofit is no small feat. It's a journey filled with excitement, purpose, and fulfillment but also one of immense complexity and overwhelming challenges. For me, it was a pivotal undertaking—an opportunity to transform my vision into a reality capable of creating meaningful change for the MS community. At the same time, it required me to navigate an entirely new world of regulations, paperwork, and strategic planning, all while managing my health. Stress is a serious trigger of my MS symptoms, so my approach to building the nonprofit had to be intentional. I knew I needed guidance, support, and a community to help bring Locke's Promise to life without compromising my well-being. And if you know me, you know that when I put my mind to something, it doesn't happen eventually—it happens as soon as possible.

I partnered with an organization that specializes in helping individuals establish nonprofits, knowing their insights would be invaluable in guiding me through the initial stages. Together, we worked to identify my goals and refine the overall mission of Locke's Promise. Every element was documented to create a clear foundation: Bylaws were crafted with precision, letters to the state reflected my compelling story, and projected numbers for growth and success were carefully aligned for the IRS when submitting my application for 501(c)(3) status. For anyone who wants to start a nonprofit, I strongly recommend investing in this kind of expert support to build a solid foundation for the nonprofit, preserve peace of mind, and minimize stress.

BUILDING THE RIGHT TEAM

While I thrive on challenges and hard work, I also understand my limitations, and I knew I couldn't tackle every aspect of building a nonprofit alone. I leaned into the expertise of professionals to streamline the process and ensure that every detail was handled correctly. The next step was hiring a web designer specializing in nonprofit platforms to help create the Locke's Promise website (www.lockespromise.com). While I have experience (and even enjoy) designing other websites, I recognized the unique needs of a nonprofit site and wanted to ensure it met those standards.

From the beginning, I understood that a nonprofit website needed to go beyond standard web design—it had to incorporate secure donation processing, ensure tax exemption compliance, maintain financial transparency, and emphasize storytelling and advocacy. I wanted to create a site that would meet these essential standards and serve as a trusted platform for fundraising, engagement, and community impact.

Next, I brought on a public relations expert to help build my brand and amplify my message. I knew that effectively sharing my story and mission would be key to garnering support and inspiring the community to rally behind Locke's Promise. With the PR professional's help, I began spreading the word about the nonprofit and its vision for empowering and uplifting those living with MS. In addition to their help, I also leaned on an old colleague and friend who had experience writing press releases and bios. They helped me hone in on the key aspects of my message and draft pitch letters to the press, press releases of varying lengths, and other essential materials to officially announce the launch of Locke's Promise.

As the organization took shape, I hired an accountant to handle the financial complexities. From running the numbers to projecting budgets for growth, they became an integral part of ensuring Locke's Promise would thrive both in the short and long term.

Beyond hiring professionals, I leaned into my community even further. I contacted trusted friends, colleagues, and connections, forming a strong board of directors who shared my passion and commitment. This group became the backbone of Locke's Promise, offering guidance, insight, and unwavering support as we began our work. My board of directors is a testament to the strength of my community and my commitment to our mission. It's composed of my closest friends— trusted allies who are always ready to lend a hand—alongside two others living with MS, providing invaluable shared experiences and perspectives. Rounding out this powerhouse team is someone I fondly call my MS gold card member, my trusted MS specialist and dear friend, Dr. Ann Cabot. Together, this diverse and dedicated group brings the perfect blend of support, expertise, and passion to ensure Locke's Promise achieves its mission and continues to thrive.

With this incredible team in place, I had all the right players to turn my vision into a resounding success. I couldn't have asked for a better group of people to stand alongside me as we work to make a lasting impact on the MS community.

LEARNING THE NONPROFIT WORLD

Starting a nonprofit wasn't just about building infrastructure—it was also about immersing myself in the world of nonprofit management. I threw myself into learning everything I could, from charitable giving strategies to networking with organizations that shared my mission. I made phone calls, introducing myself to as many nonprofit leaders and philanthropic foundations as possible. My goal was simple—learning how to help each other and create lasting partnerships.

There are trials and tribulations to everything, and that includes the nonprofit world. I have learned some fundraising do's and don'ts on my own, but wouldn't we all have to experience the don'ts? That is why networking and introducing yourself to others who have done it and already have learned is key. Meeting numerous nonprofit founders, owners, and board members was essential—phone calls, Zoom meetings, and emails back and forth. Sharing ideas and listening to their stories and what their organizations do all helped me learn quickly.

I also sought online and live seminars and classes to educate myself and my board on the best practices for running a nonprofit. My motto became "fail fast and move forward," embracing mistakes as part of the learning process and refining my approach. With each conversation, class, and meeting, I grew more confident in my ability to lead Locke's Promise and create an organization that genuinely made a difference.

I know it's important never to stop growing and learning, and I will continue to evolve alongside anyone who wants to come along for the journey. If you're interested in becoming a board member, volunteering, or making an impact, don't hesitate to reach out. Locke's Promise is always looking for those willing to lean in and help the cause!

THE POWER OF COMMUNITY

Building Locke's Promise was never a solo effort for me. It was a collective endeavor, relying on the expertise of professionals, the strength of my board of directors, and the unwavering support of the overall community. I firmly believe in the saying "It takes a village," and my journey is a testament to that truth.

While the process was far from easy, my determination, combined with the wisdom and assistance of those around me, turned a daunting vision into a tangible reality. Locke's Promise stands as proof that with the right resources, a clear mission, and a strong team, even the most overwhelming challenges can be overcome.

My advice to others considering starting a nonprofit is impactful yet straightforward: Invest in your future, protect your mental and emotional health, and build a community that shares your passion. The journey may be difficult, but the results—and the impact—are worth every step.

Chapter 15

WHEN LOVE WEARS THIN: CAREGIVER FATIGUE AND THE GUILT THAT FOLLOWS

We can't tell the full story without acknowledging the ones who stand strong behind it—the unwavering supporters, the steady shoulders to lean on. These are the people in a person with MS's life who show up when the rest of the world fades into the background. The ones who offer comfort, strength, and unshakable care—because their love and commitment make all the difference. Behind every person navigating life with MS, there's a silent pillar of strength—the care partners and loved ones who stand beside us when the disease tries to pull us apart. While the term *caregiver* is often used, many individuals living with MS feel that it implies dependency in a way that doesn't fully reflect their experience. Especially when it's a spouse, close friend, or family member, *care partner* is a term that acknowledges mutual support rather than one-sided care.

It's easy to focus on the person diagnosed, but MS doesn't just impact one individual—it ripples through families, reshaping routines, shifting relationships, and introducing challenges that few ever anticipate. The journey isn't just about managing symptoms; it's about preserving autonomy, dignity, and the bonds that keep life moving forward.

THE CAREPARTNER'S JOURNEY: A ROLE NOBODY TRAINS FOR

Carepartners come in many forms—spouses, partners, parents, children, close friends—each stepping in where needed, often without warning or preparation. They become chauffeurs, nurses, emotional lifelines, handling daily tasks like bathing, dressing, managing medical appointments, and offering unwavering support through flare-ups and setbacks.

The hardest part? MS is wildly unpredictable. Symptoms can hit suddenly, forcing carepartners into action without notice. It's an exhausting cycle, a constant state of readiness that can lead to burnout, as carepartners pour everything into supporting their loved one while often neglecting their personal needs.

WHEN MS SHIFTS THE FAMILY DYNAMIC

For families, MS isn't just a diagnosis—it's a new reality. Spouses and partners may transition from equal partners to primary carepartners, a shift that can strain relationships and create feelings of isolation. I personally know that when this takes place, for me, I am not going to take it sitting down, I am going to fight it. I want to be as independent as possible for as long as possible and beyond. No one wants to be cared for. Even the pushing back during this phase can be hard on the carepartner, as all they are trying to do is support and love. What I currently experience are mood swings. MS can bring intense emotional shifts that bubble up like a volcano with no shutoff valve. There's even a term for it: pseudobulbar affect, a condition where uncontrollable emotions take center stage. It's not intentional, but it happens and can test even the strongest bonds. I typically keep a fierce filter on during the work day to make sure I come off as pleasant as possible however at the end of a long day where I have been on the verge of an emotional breakdown, those that end up experiencing it are my loved ones, right here at home.

Children experience challenges. Watching a parent struggle with symptoms can be confusing and heartbreaking, especially when MS is invisible on the outside but still creates internal barriers. When a parent looks fine but isn't, communication becomes critical—kids need honest conversations, reassurance, and an open space to process what they don't always understand. I find that I have to be super clear with my daughter about when I need help and when I want to try to do it on my own. Because she is currently sixteen, she doesn't jump at helping at much and definitely waits for me to explicitly ask for it and explain the exact reason I need her help—and it better be a good reason!

Even extended family and friends can struggle to offer support. Because MS is often invisible, people might underestimate its impact, unintentionally dismissing the struggles of both the person diagnosed and the family supporting them.

RESILIENCE, AWARENESS, AND THE POWER OF COMMUNITY

Carepartners and families should never stand in the shadows. Their stories are ones of incredible strength, navigating the hardships, uncertainty, and sacrifices that come with supporting a loved one through MS. Despite the challenges, many find purpose and deepened bonds, proving that love has no limits when tested.

That's why building awareness and support matters. Through Locke's Promise, I'm working to highlight these unsung heroes, offering resources, education, and solidarity for families affected by MS in New Hampshire and everywhere.

With events, workshops, and support groups, Locke's Promise fosters understanding, encourages conversations about the invisible nature of MS, and ensures that carepartners and families feel seen, validated, and supported.

By creating a movement centered on visibility and empowerment, we're paving the way for stronger communities, more open conversations, and a future where no one faces MS alone.

The journey of MS is rarely a solo one. Alongside every person facing the disease, there is often a care partner—a spouse, a sibling, a close friend—someone whose quiet strength provides stability when the ground feels unsteady. Their role is invaluable yet easily overlooked.

To every carepartner reading this, you may not wear a cape, but you are a hero nonetheless. Take care of you, too—you matter just as much as the person you're holding up.

This one's for the unsung heroes—the ones who give endlessly, take the emotional hits, and somehow still manage to keep smiling (even if it's through gritted teeth). Their well-being matters just as much as the person they support. And yes, they'll likely be met with resistance, frustration, and the occasional stubborn refusal to accept help. But trust us, it's not about you—it's about the gut-punch of realizing independence doesn't come as easily as it used to. Whether it's at twenty-eight, thirty-five, fifty-nine, or seventy, admitting we need help is tough. So if we grumble, roll our eyes, or act like we can do it all alone, just know that deep down, we appreciate you (even if we don't say it out loud).

Chapter 16

EXPANDING IMPACT: FROM CLIMBING TO GOLFING TO JEEPING

Climbing the Peak for MS has always been a cornerstone of my journey, as I have consistently channeled funds toward the National MS Society (NMSS) to drive progress toward a cure. The climbing event's mission remains steadfast, ensuring research and advocacy efforts continue to thrive. However, with the establishment of Locke's Promise, I recognized the need to expand my reach and create a complementary event that could support both organizations in unique ways.

Unknowingly, the answer had already parked itself in my driveway. Just months before my diagnosis, I had purchased my Jeep, drawn to its rugged spirit and adventurous possibilities. At the time, I had no idea how pivotal this vehicle would become in my life. As hiking fell out of reach, my Jeep offered me a new way to explore, challenge myself, and reignite my passion for adventure.

It wasn't long before an idea sparked. Inspired by the bold and supportive nature of the Jeep community, I envisioned an event that would harness this energy to raise awareness and funds for MS. The Jeep world, built on camaraderie and resilience, was the perfect platform to rally people behind the cause. And so, Rides & Wranglers for MS was born—a sister event designed to provide additional proceeds to NMSS and lay the foundation for Locke's Promise's grant fund.

This initiative directly aids those living with MS by addressing immediate needs and covering essential (and often overlooked) operational costs needed to sustain and grow the nonprofit's impact.

The event embodies everything I love—adventure, community, and advocacy. Jeep enthusiasts from across the region come together to showcase their rides—whether stock, fully modified, the dirtiest, or the oldest—all while raising funds and awareness for MS. Much like Climb the Peak for MS, Rides & Wranglers for MS is more than just a fundraiser— it's a celebration of resilience. It proves that life can still be bold, exciting, and filled with connection even in the face of adversity.

And why climb or jeep when you can golf? We added a third event to the mix to capture the attention of the golfing community—an opportunity to bring people together for a cause that truly matters. Golf provides a relaxed yet competitive setting where players can enjoy the sport they love while supporting the fight against MS. This event isn't just about hitting the green; it's about raising awareness, funding critical research, and fostering a sense of community among those affected by MS. By engaging golf enthusiasts, sponsors, and supporters, we've expanded our mission beyond outdoor adventures, creating an inclusive way for people to give back, connect, and make an impact. Whether swinging a club or showing support from the sidelines, every contribution helps push us closer to a future without MS—one stroke at a time.

Together, these three events—Climb the Peak for MS; Rides & Wranglers for MS; and MS Golf Classic, Swinging For A Cure—form a powerful trio, driving hope, support, and resources for the MS community.

The Jeep trails have become my new mountains, and with every bump in the road, I keep moving forward, proving once again that the power of connection and determination can overcome anything.

Climb the Peak for MS, 2023

MS Golf Classic, Swinging for a Cure, 2025

Rides & Wranglers for MS, 2025

Chapter 17

EMBRACING THE JOURNEY

As I sit here, weaving together the threads of my story, I am struck by the weight of every moment that has led me to this exact place—every challenge, every triumph, every aching uncertainty. Writing this book is not just about documenting my journey; it is about feeling it all over again, reliving the joy, grief, transformation, and raw resilience that have carried me forward. Life has tested me in ways I never saw coming—through the complexities of motherhood, the courage of coming out, and the uncharted terrain of living with MS. Each chapter has reshaped me, molding my perspective, stretching my limits, and revealing depths of strength I didn't know existed. And yet, through the uncertainty, the setbacks, the quiet moments of doubt, one truth has never wavered: I move forward. Always. Not because it's easy but because I refuse to let life's hardships define me—I define myself.

MY "WHY"

My daughter is at the heart of everything I do—every struggle I overcome, every choice I make. She is my northstar, my reason to keep going even when life feels impossibly heavy. I often refer to her as my "why." Why keep moving? For her. Why not fall apart? For her. Why choose to embrace change even when it feels terrifying? For her.

She came into this world under extraordinary circumstances—a high-risk pregnancy, born early at just thirty-three weeks. My body has always tended to reject the foreign, attacking itself in ways I couldn't control. Her existence, a miracle against the odds, changed everything. As I faced my health struggles and ultimately underwent a hysterectomy, her presence in my life became even more profound.

Our bond is unbreakable, rooted in love and an understanding that transcends words. She feels my pain deeply, sometimes too deeply. When I cry, she cries. She senses the struggles I try so hard to shield her from. While this empathy is a testament to her beautiful heart, I must ensure she never carries the weight of my challenges alone.

I strive to be her example of strength and resilience but also her safe space—a mother who leads with honesty yet offers her daughter the security to grow without fear. She reminds me daily of my purpose and power to keep pushing forward.

NAVIGATING GUILT AND GRACE

Coming out as gay when my daughter was just six years old was one of the hardest decisions I've ever made. It shattered the life we had built, a reality that was comfortable but not fully honest. My ex-husband—an incredible man with an unwavering kindness—stood by me, offering support when I needed it most. Still, the guilt weighed heavily on me. I questioned whether I was doing enough, whether I had disrupted my daughter's sense of security.

But I also knew that living authentically was the only way I could be the mother she truly deserved. I wanted her to grow up knowing that embracing who you are, even when it's hard, is worth it. And while the transition wasn't easy, love remained central to our family dynamic. My ex-husband and I worked together to ensure our daughter felt safe, supported, and deeply loved despite the changes.

STRENGTH IN VULNERABILITY

Motherhood is challenging on its own, but adding MS into the equation has forced me to redefine what it means to be strong. Some days, my body feels like it's betraying me—fatigue sets in too quickly, pain lingers longer than I want, and uncertainty is always present. But even on my hardest days, I remind myself that showing up for my daughter isn't about perfection; it's about presence.

There have been moments when I've had to adapt—shifting our routines, making space for rest when my body demands it. But I've never let MS dictate the quality of our time together. Whether playing games, sharing stories, or just holding her close, I ensure she knows how deeply she is loved.

A SHARED JOURNEY

Through it all, my daughter and I have navigated this life together—learning, growing, and discovering resilience in ways neither of us expected. We've had hard and beautiful days, but no matter what, we move forward hand in hand. She has been my greatest source of inspiration, reminding me there is always something to fight for despite adversity.

Motherhood isn't just about holding it all together—it's about creating a life filled with love, authenticity, and hope. While this road has been far from easy, I wouldn't trade it for anything. And as my journey continues, I know that with courage and love as my guides, another chapter is always waiting to be written.

DRIVING FORWARD—THE ROAD AHEAD

Adversity is an inevitable part of life, shaping us in ways we may not expect. Whether it's the fear and vulnerability of coming out as queer or the daily battles of living with an invisible, incurable disease like MS, challenges surround us all. They test our limits, challenge our sense of self, and push us to places we never thought we'd go. But within those struggles lies an opportunity to overcome, grow, and learn acceptance for ourselves and our journey. It's not easy, and it often takes time, but by facing adversity head-on and embracing the strength we find along the way, we can rise above and create lives rooted in resilience and authenticity.

The future is always uncertain, but if there's one thing I've proven, it's that determination, resilience, and community can overcome even the steepest challenges. What started as a deeply personal journey has grown into a movement that inspires hope and action. Through Locke's Promise, I've laid a foundation for raising awareness, funding research, and creating meaningful change in those living with MS.

Looking ahead, I'm more determined than ever to drive the mission of Locke's Promise forward. There's still so much work to be done, and I'm ready to grow my nonprofit's events, donor audience, and impact.

Through it all, I remain steadfast in my ultimate goal—to make the world free of MS. I understand the power of collective effort—that every dollar raised, every conversation started, and every event hosted brings us one step closer to a cure. But just as importantly, I'm committed to helping individuals today, whether it's by making their lives more accessible, easing their financial burdens, or simply being a source of understanding and empathy.

I know the road won't always be smooth, but I also know I have the strength, the network, and the motivation to keep moving forward. Locke's Promise is no longer just a vision—it's a driving force for change, fueled by the belief that MS ends with us.

As I look to the horizon, I do so with hope and determination, ready to continue climbing, driving, and forging a path toward a brighter future for the MS community. Because no one should ever face MS alone, and together, we'll make the world stronger, kinder, and free of MS.

Chapter 18

WORDS TO INSPIRE AND EMPOWER

Throughout my journey, one thing has always stood out—the power of words to uplift, motivate, and ignite change. Quotes and messages of empowerment have been my lifeline during the darkest days and my rallying cry during the brightest. They've given me strength when the weight of the world felt unbearable and helped me find clarity when the path seemed uncertain.

Empowering words have a unique way of resonating deeply, reminding us that we are capable, resilient, and never truly alone. They encourage us to embrace our vulnerabilities, recognize our inner strength, and take even the smallest steps toward progress. They remind us that while life may be unpredictable and challenging, we are always more powerful than we realize.

Here are a few taglines I live by:

- Put everything that you have into everything that you do.
- Success is a journey, not a destination.
- Your story is your strength; tell it well and tell it often.

Here are some words of inspiration that have guided me along the way:

- "I can be changed by what happens to me, but I refuse to be reduced by it."—A reminder that challenges shape us, but they don't define us.
- "Go easy on yourself. Whatever you accomplish today, let it be enough."—A lesson in self-compassion and the importance of celebrating small victories.
- "Strength doesn't come from what you can do. It comes from overcoming the things you once thought you couldn't."—Proof that resilience is built step by step.

These simple yet profound words offer solace and a call to action—a reminder that within every individual lies the power to overcome, adapt, and thrive. My story has shown that the smallest actions, the quietest strength, and the softest words can have the biggest impact.

Let these messages be your guide. Whether you're climbing your own mountains or looking to support someone else on their journey, remember that you, too, can create change, spread hope, and leave a lasting legacy.

MY CLOSING THOUGHTS

As I bring this book to a close, I want to reflect on what this journey has meant for me and, hopefully, for you as well. Life is a complex, unpredictable, and sometimes relentless force. It throws challenges at us that we didn't see coming and offers lessons we never thought we needed to learn. For me, it's been about finding strength in vulnerability, courage in authenticity, and purpose through adversity.

My story is one of many. It's unique to me, yet I hope you've found pieces of it that resonate, moments that feel familiar, and truths that speak to your journey. Whether navigating a life-changing diagnosis, embracing your true self, or simply trying to find your footing in a world that can feel overwhelming, I hope this book has reminded you of one thing: You are not alone.

If there's anything I've learned, it's that the most beautiful and transformative parts of life often come from the hardest struggles. It takes time, patience, and a willingness to show up for yourself—even when it feels impossible. But through it all, there is always hope.

This book isn't just about me; it's about connection. It's about reaching out, sharing stories, and reminding ourselves that we're all in this together. I hope these chapters have inspired you to look at your challenges with fresh eyes, seek the strength that's always been within you, and embrace the imperfect, beautiful truth of who you are.

Thank you for allowing me to share my story with you. Let's continue to uplift one another, be allies in each other's journeys, and spread kindness, understanding, and love wherever possible. After all, the world could always use a little more of it.

With gratitude, understanding, and hope,

Sarah Locke

Sarah and her hiking tribe at the Summit of Mount Washington, June 2020

Reaching the Summit, June 2020

Sarah, Summer 2022

Sarah and her partner, Summer 2022

Sarah at the Spartan Race, Summer 2015

Sarah at the Summit of Mount Major, Summer 2020

Sarah and her anchor and friend, Summer 2018

Sarah sits directly in the water to cool off when hiking, Summer 2021

Sarah and her anchor and friend, Summer 2018

Sarah and her anchor and friend, June 2020

Sarah with her daughter and partner at Climb the Peak for MS, 2024

Sarah's partner, daughter, and Zephyr, Summer 2023

Sarah with her dad, mom, daughter, and partner, 2025

ABOUT THE AUTHOR

Energetic, passionate, and driven, Sarah Locke is a dynamic force in the social media marketing world. As a social media strategist at Dell Technologies, Sarah leads digital marketing initiatives and serves as a subject matter expert in social media strategy, specializing in partner ecosystem messaging.

Beyond her professional endeavors, Sarah is a mother, fitness enthusiast, and MS advocate—a role she proudly embraces after her diagnosis in 2019. In 2023, Sarah founded the Climb the Peak for MS event at Pats Peak Ski Area in Henniker, New Hampshire, to build awareness and raise funds to find a cure for multiple sclerosis. She became an MS Ambassador to create as many opportunities as possible to talk about MS, share her story, and raise research funds to find a cure in her lifetime. She also produces and hosts her podcast, Your Story is Your Strength. In 2025, Sarah added two new events to her fundraising efforts: the MS Golf Classic, Swinging for a Cure, in August at the Stonebridge Country

Club in Goffstown, New Hampshire, and Rides & Wranglers for MS in September at Anheuser-Busch in Merrimack, New Hampshire.

Sarah has also started her own non-profit organization to further her dedication and commitment to finding a cure for MS. As president and CEO of Locke's Promise, Sarah brings a powerful personal story and mission to the forefront of MS awareness and advocacy. Her goal with Locke's Promise is to not only raise funds but also build a supportive community for those living with MS in New Hampshire and New England. She hopes the community will help to provide guidance, resources, and grants to help those affected by MS live a fulfilled day-to-day life while waiting for a cure for this invisible disease. Her tagline is Never MS Alone. We are here to listen, lean on, and lift!

With a BS in marketing and an MBA from Clarkson University, Sarah understands the power of social media not only as a tool for business but as a platform for storytelling, connection, and personal branding. Whether she's sharing industry insights, attending exclusive events on behalf of Dell Technologies, promoting her MS fundraising, or highlighting moments with family and friends, Sarah seamlessly integrates her expertise with her personal life.

When she's not immersed in digital strategy, you'll find Sarah embracing the outdoors—hiking and kayaking with her partner, and most importantly, spending time with her daughter, her ultimate "why." Her boundless energy and unwavering positivity fuel both her career and personal journey.

www.ingramcontent.com/pod-product-compliance
Lightning Source LLC
Chambersburg PA
CBHW021204130626
46554CB00005B/1980